★★★★★★★★★★★★ HARCOURT HORIZONS

United States History,

Canada, Mexico, & Central America

Activity Book

Teacher's Edition

Orlando   Austin   Chicago   NewYork   Toronto   London   San Diego

Visit *The Learning Site!*
www.harcourtschool.com

ISBN 0-15-335843-2

1 2 3 4 5 6 7 8 9 10 073 10 09 08 07 06 05 04 03 02

The activities in this book reinforce social studies concepts and skills in **Harcourt Horizons: United States History, Canada, Mexico, & Central America.** There is one activity for every lesson and skill in the Pupil Edition. There is also a two-page activity for every Compare/Contrast section that appears at the end of each unit. Copies of the activity pages appear with answers in the Teacher's Edition. In addition to activities, this book also contains reproductions of the graphic organizers that appear in the Chapter Reviews in the Pupil Edition. Multiple-choice test preparation pages for student practice are also provided. A blank multiple-choice answer sheet can be found after these contents pages.

Contents

Introduction

·UNIT·

1

Chapter 1

Chapter 2

Name ____________________ Date ____________

Multiple-Choice Answer Sheet

Number your answers to match the questions on the test page.

____ Ⓐ Ⓑ Ⓒ Ⓓ

____ Ⓕ Ⓖ Ⓗ Ⓙ

____ Ⓐ Ⓑ Ⓒ Ⓓ

____ Ⓕ Ⓖ Ⓗ Ⓙ

____ Ⓐ Ⓑ Ⓒ Ⓓ

____ Ⓐ Ⓑ Ⓒ Ⓓ

____ Ⓕ Ⓖ Ⓗ Ⓙ

____ Ⓐ Ⓑ Ⓒ Ⓓ

____ Ⓕ Ⓖ Ⓗ Ⓙ

____ Ⓐ Ⓑ Ⓒ Ⓓ

____ Ⓐ Ⓑ Ⓒ Ⓓ

____ Ⓕ Ⓖ Ⓗ Ⓙ

____ Ⓐ Ⓑ Ⓒ Ⓓ

____ Ⓕ Ⓖ Ⓗ Ⓙ

____ Ⓐ Ⓑ Ⓒ Ⓓ

____ Ⓐ Ⓑ Ⓒ Ⓓ

____ Ⓕ Ⓖ Ⓗ Ⓙ

____ Ⓐ Ⓑ Ⓒ Ⓓ

____ Ⓕ Ⓖ Ⓗ Ⓙ

____ Ⓐ Ⓑ Ⓒ Ⓓ

____ Ⓐ Ⓑ Ⓒ Ⓓ

____ Ⓕ Ⓖ Ⓗ Ⓙ

____ Ⓐ Ⓑ Ⓒ Ⓓ

____ Ⓕ Ⓖ Ⓗ Ⓙ

____ Ⓐ Ⓑ Ⓒ Ⓓ

____ Ⓐ Ⓑ Ⓒ Ⓓ

____ Ⓕ Ⓖ Ⓗ Ⓙ

____ Ⓐ Ⓑ Ⓒ Ⓓ

____ Ⓕ Ⓖ Ⓗ Ⓙ

____ Ⓐ Ⓑ Ⓒ Ⓓ

____ Ⓐ Ⓑ Ⓒ Ⓓ

____ Ⓕ Ⓖ Ⓗ Ⓙ

____ Ⓐ Ⓑ Ⓒ Ⓓ

____ Ⓕ Ⓖ Ⓗ Ⓙ

____ Ⓐ Ⓑ Ⓒ Ⓓ

____ Ⓐ Ⓑ Ⓒ Ⓓ

____ Ⓕ Ⓖ Ⓗ Ⓙ

____ Ⓐ Ⓑ Ⓒ Ⓓ

____ Ⓕ Ⓖ Ⓗ Ⓙ

____ Ⓐ Ⓑ Ⓒ Ⓓ

____ Ⓐ Ⓑ Ⓒ Ⓓ

____ Ⓕ Ⓖ Ⓗ Ⓙ

____ Ⓐ Ⓑ Ⓒ Ⓓ

____ Ⓕ Ⓖ Ⓗ Ⓙ

____ Ⓐ Ⓑ Ⓒ Ⓓ

____ Ⓐ Ⓑ Ⓒ Ⓓ

____ Ⓕ Ⓖ Ⓗ Ⓙ

____ Ⓐ Ⓑ Ⓒ Ⓓ

____ Ⓕ Ⓖ Ⓗ Ⓙ

____ Ⓐ Ⓑ Ⓒ Ⓓ

____ Ⓐ Ⓑ Ⓒ Ⓓ

____ Ⓕ Ⓖ Ⓗ Ⓙ

____ Ⓐ Ⓑ Ⓒ Ⓓ

____ Ⓕ Ⓖ Ⓗ Ⓙ

____ Ⓐ Ⓑ Ⓒ Ⓓ

____ Ⓐ Ⓑ Ⓒ Ⓓ

____ Ⓕ Ⓖ Ⓗ Ⓙ

____ Ⓐ Ⓑ Ⓒ Ⓓ

____ Ⓕ Ⓖ Ⓗ Ⓙ

____ Ⓐ Ⓑ Ⓒ Ⓓ

____ Ⓐ Ⓑ Ⓒ Ⓓ

____ Ⓕ Ⓖ Ⓗ Ⓙ

____ Ⓐ Ⓑ Ⓒ Ⓓ

____ Ⓕ Ⓖ Ⓗ Ⓙ

____ Ⓐ Ⓑ Ⓒ Ⓓ

____ Ⓐ Ⓑ Ⓒ Ⓓ

____ Ⓕ Ⓖ Ⓗ Ⓙ

____ Ⓐ Ⓑ Ⓒ Ⓓ

____ Ⓕ Ⓖ Ⓗ Ⓙ

____ Ⓐ Ⓑ Ⓒ Ⓓ

____ Ⓐ Ⓑ Ⓒ Ⓓ

____ Ⓕ Ⓖ Ⓗ Ⓙ

____ Ⓐ Ⓑ Ⓒ Ⓓ

____ Ⓕ Ⓖ Ⓗ Ⓙ

____ Ⓐ Ⓑ Ⓒ Ⓓ

____ Ⓐ Ⓑ Ⓒ Ⓓ

____ Ⓕ Ⓖ Ⓗ Ⓙ

____ Ⓐ Ⓑ Ⓒ Ⓓ

____ Ⓕ Ⓖ Ⓗ Ⓙ

____ Ⓐ Ⓑ Ⓒ Ⓓ

____ Ⓐ Ⓑ Ⓒ Ⓓ

____ Ⓕ Ⓖ Ⓗ Ⓙ

____ Ⓐ Ⓑ Ⓒ Ⓓ

____ Ⓕ Ⓖ Ⓗ Ⓙ

____ Ⓐ Ⓑ Ⓒ Ⓓ

____ Ⓐ Ⓑ Ⓒ Ⓓ

____ Ⓕ Ⓖ Ⓗ Ⓙ

____ Ⓐ Ⓑ Ⓒ Ⓓ

____ Ⓕ Ⓖ Ⓗ Ⓙ

____ Ⓐ Ⓑ Ⓒ Ⓓ

Name _____ Date _____

MAP AND GLOBE SKILLS

Read a Map

Directions Use the map to answer the questions that follow.

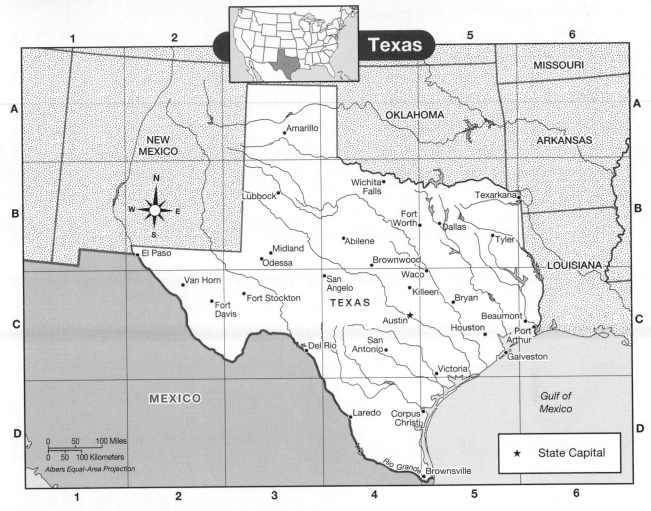

1. What is the capital of Texas? Austin

2. What states border Texas? New Mexico, Oklahoma, Arkansas, Louisiana

3. What cities are located in C5? Waco, Bryan, Houston, Victoria, Galveston

4. What bodies of water border Texas? the Gulf of Mexico and the Rio Grande

5. About how many miles is it from Fort Davis to El Paso if you drive through

   Van Horn? about 170 mi.

   What direction do you travel to get there? NW

6. What river forms the border between Texas and Mexico? the Rio Grande

Name ____________________ Date ____________

Why History Matters

Directions **Use the terms in the Word Bank to complete the sentences below.**

history	oral history	historical empathy	analyze
chronology	point of view	frames of reference	

1. People's ___frames of reference___ are based on where people were when an event happened and how they were involved with that event.

2. ___chronology___ is the order in which events happened.

3. A person's ___point of view___ is based on his or her age, gender, class, background, and experiences.

4. Historians listen to and read records of ___oral history___ to help them understand past events.

5. Understanding ___history___ helps you understand the present.

Name _____ Date _____

Compare Primary and Secondary Sources

Directions Use Captain Charles Sigsbee's letter and the *New York Times* article to answer the questions below.

The New York Times.

The *Maine* Blown Up

Terrible Explosion on Board the United States Battleship
in Havana Harbor
MANY PERSONS KILLED AND WOUNDED
. . . None of the Wounded Men Able to Give Any
Explanation of the Cause of the Disaster

Havana, Feb. 15—At 9:45 o'clock this evening a terrible explosion took place on board the United States battleship *Maine* in Havana Harbor.

Many persons were killed or wounded. All the boats of the Spanish cruiser *Alfonso XII* are assisting.

As yet the cause of the explosion is not *apparent*. The wounded sailors of the *Maine* are unable to explain it. It is believed that the battleship is totally destroyed. . . .

"... I felt the crash of the explosion. It was a ... roar of immense volume, largely metallic in character. It was succeeded by a ... trembling and lurching motion of the vessel, then ... an eclipse of the electric lights and intense darkness within the cabin. I knew immediately that the MAINE had been blown up and that she was sinking ...."

Captain Charles D. Sigsbee,
MAINE Commanding Officer

1 What source lists where the explosion occurred? the newspaper article _____

2 How did Captain Sigsbee know the *Maine* was sinking?

He felt the ship trembling and lurching and saw the lights go out. _____

3 What does Captain Sigsbee's letter tell you that the *New York Times* article

does not? Captain Sigsbee's letter describes what it felt like inside the ship. ____

4 How is the tone of the newspaper article different from the tone of the letter?

The newspaper article is more factual, with less emotion. _____

Why Geography Matters

Geography is the study of the Earth's surface and the way people use it. Geographers use many different themes and topics to study a place. Understanding these themes and topics and their relationships will help you to better understand geography.

Directions **Use the Word Bank to fill in the web and the question below.**

Places and Regions	Geography	Location
Movement	Human Feature	Uses of Geography
Environment and Society	Human Systems	Physical Feature

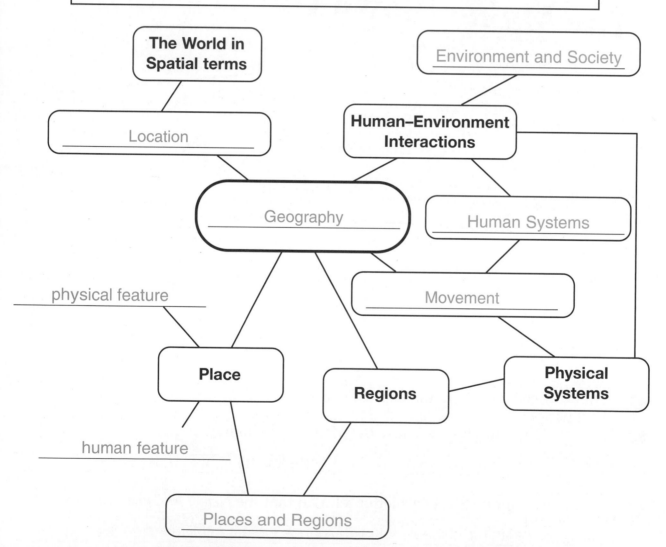

Knowing how to use maps, globes, and geographic tools helps you understand the

_____ uses of geography _____ and prepares you for life.

Why Economics, Civics, and Government Matter

Directions Read the flow chart and answer the questions below.

Consumers pay taxes on
goods and services.

Civics

Those taxes are paid
to the government.

Consumers buy goods
and services.

$

Government

Economics

The government uses taxes to
provide services, build roads,
and fund education.

From their jobs, workers
earn money, which they can
spend on various goods
and services.

Government programs
create various jobs.

1 What happens when fewer jobs are available and unemployment goes up?
Consumers have less money and buy fewer goods and services, fewer
taxes are paid, and the government has less money to provide services.

2 What step happens between when the government creates jobs and when
consumers buy goods and services? Workers earn money which they can use
to buy goods and services.

3 What happens when the government raises taxes? The government has more
money to provide services, but consumers may not be able to afford to buy as
much.

4 What would happen if consumers did not pay taxes on goods and services?
The government would not have that money to provide services, build roads,
and fund education.

Land and Regions

Directions Look at each numbered place on the map. Find the word in the box that describes the place. Then write the word on the line with the same number.

sea level	basin	mountain range	plain
valley	volcano	piedmont	plateau

1 _____volcano_____

2 ____mountain range____

3 _____valley_____

4 _____plateau_____

5 _____plain_____

6 _____sea level_____

Directions Show the meaning of the words *piedmont* and *plateau* by using each word in a sentence.

A piedmont is the area at or near the foot of a mountain. A plateau is a flat area

that stands high above the surrounding land.

_____

© Harcourt

Name _____ Date _____

MAP AND GLOBE SKILLS
Use Elevation Maps

Directions Study the elevation map and answer the questions below.

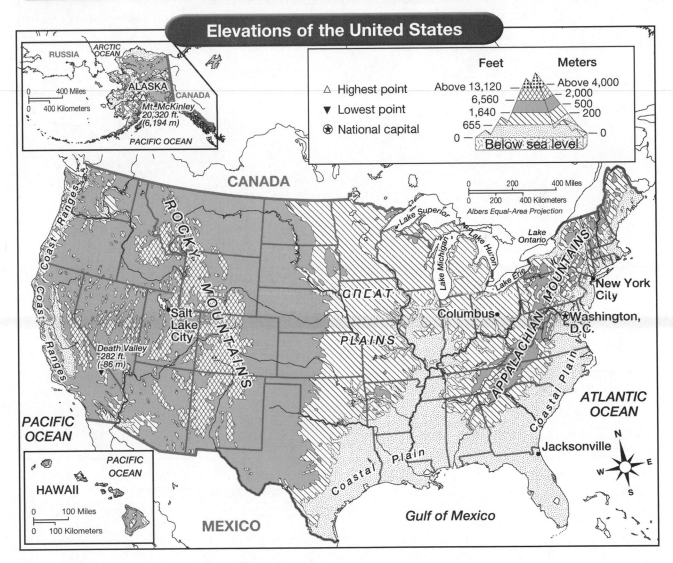

Elevations of the United States

1 Which city has the higher elevation: Jacksonville, Florida, or Columbus, Ohio?

Columbus, Ohio

2 What is the elevation range of the Rocky Mountains? from 6,560 ft. to above

13,120 ft. (from 2,000 m to 4,000 m)

3 In what state can you find an inland location that is lower than sea level? What is

the name of the location? Death Valley in California

Use after reading Chapter 1, Skill Lesson, pages 24–25.

Name _____   Date _____

Bodies of Water

Directions Use the map to answer the questions below.

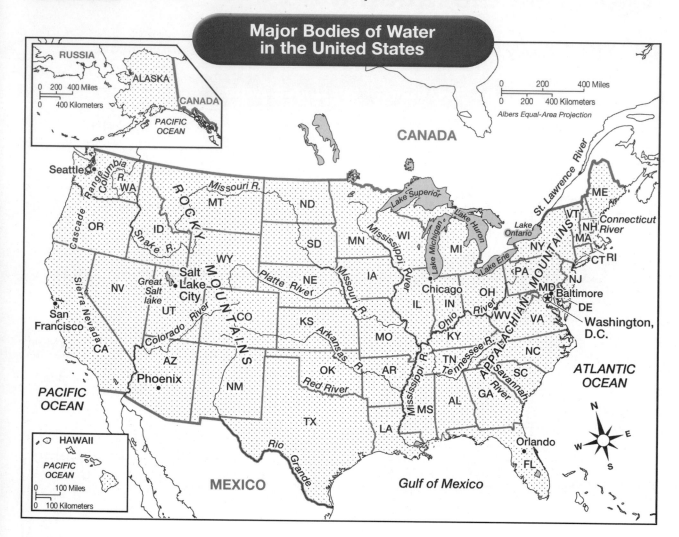

Major Bodies of Water in the United States

1 Name the Great Lakes. Lake Superior, Lake Michigan, Lake Huron, Lake Erie, Lake Ontario

2 Name the states that border the Gulf of Mexico. Texas, Louisiana, Mississippi, Alabama, Florida

3 Name three tributaries of the Mississippi River. possible answers: Missouri, Ohio, Arkansas Rivers

4 What states does the Arkansas River flow through? Arkansas, Oklahoma, Kansas, and Colorado

Use after reading Chapter 1, Lesson 2, pages 26–32.

© Harcourt

Climate and Vegetation Regions

Directions Use the map to fill in the chart below.

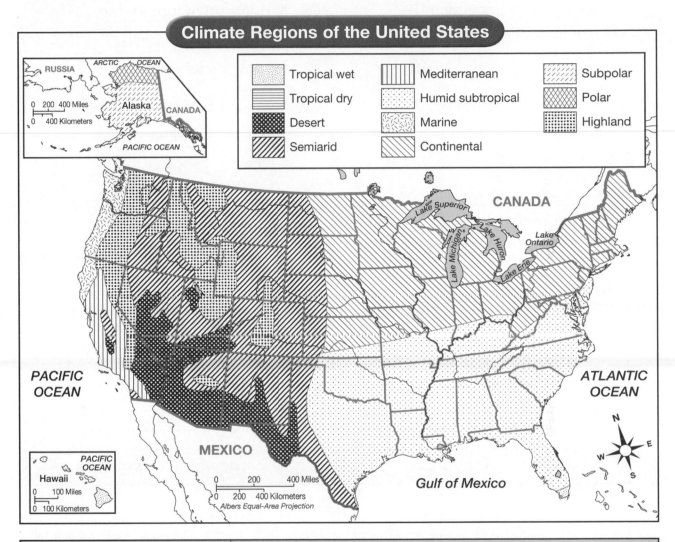

Climate Regions of the United States

Place or Region	Climate Region
Southeastern United States	humid subtropical, tropical wet
Southwestern United States	desert, semiarid, highland, humid subtropical
Pacific Coast	Mediterranean, marine, semiarid, desert
Atlantic Coast	tropical wet, humid subtropical, continental
Alaska	polar, subpolar
Hawaii	tropical wet

Use after reading Chapter 1, Lesson 3, pages 33–39.

Name _____ Date _____

Using the Land

Directions Write the correct answer in the space provided.

1 When people change their environment, they _____ modify _____ it.

2 A resource that cannot be made again by nature or people is called a _____ nonrenewable _____ resource.

3 A _____ renewable _____ resource is one that can be made again by nature or by people.

4 Farmers often modify the soil by adding _____ fertilizer _____ to grow better crops.

5 Some farmers modify their land with _____ irrigation _____, which brings water to dry areas.

Directions Write the name of the resource in the correct column.

air	iron	trees	zinc	fish
sunlight	oil	natural gas	plants	limestone
water	gold	copper	coal	wind

Renewable Resources	Nonrenewable Resources
air	gold
sunlight	coal
trees	natural gas
plants	iron
water	copper
fish	zinc
wind	oil
	limestone

Use after reading Chapter 1, Lesson 4, pages 40–43.

Where People Live and Work

Directions Read each clue. Then use the clues to complete the word puzzle below.

relative location	crossroads	suburban	rural
metropolitan	railroad	farm	economic

ACROSS

3 The location of a place compared to one or more other places

5 A place where crops are raised

6 Kind of area made up of a city and its suburbs

7 A place where two roads or railroads intersect

DOWN

1 Kind of area surrounding a large city

2 A system that moves goods overland

3 Kind of area located in the country, away from cities

4 Region named for the work done or product made within it

¹S U B U R B A N

²R
³R E L A T I V ⁴E L O C A T I O N
U   I   C
R   L   O
A   R   N
L   O   O
⁵F A R M   ⁶M E T R O P O L I T A N
    D   I
    ⁷C R O S S R O A D S

© Harcourt

Name _____   Date _____

MAP AND GLOBE SKILLS
Use Latitude and Longitude

Directions Location is important to people choosing a place to live. People may choose to live and work near a coast or near a major transportation route. Use the map to fill in the chart below.

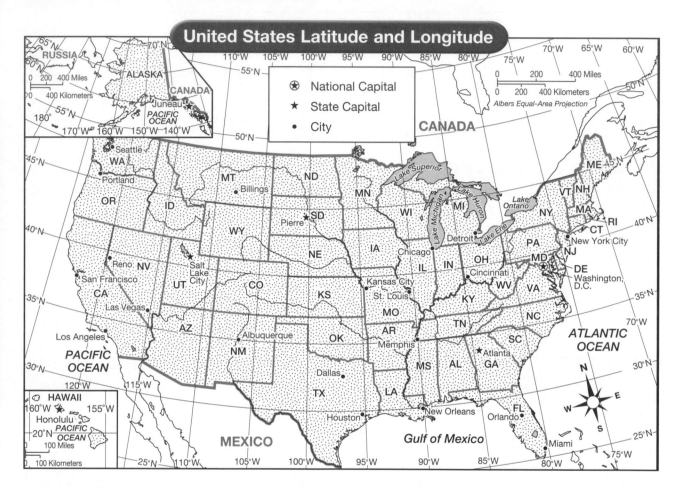

United States Latitude and Longitude

City	Latitude	Longitude
New York City, NY	41° N	74° W
Los Angeles, CA	34° N	119° W
Chicago, IL	42° N	88° W
New Orleans, LA	30° N	90° W

Use after reading Chapter 1, Skill Lesson, pages 50–51.

Name _____ Date _____

Regions of the United States

Directions Complete this graphic organizer to show that you have identified the main idea and supporting details in this chapter.

SUPPORTING DETAILS

Cultural regions reflect the customs and beliefs of the main group of people who live there.

SUPPORTING DETAILS

Economic regions are based on the work people do or the products they make.

MAIN IDEA

The United States can be divided into regions based on people's activities.

SUPPORTING DETAILS

In political regions, people share a government and have the same leaders.

SUPPORTING DETAILS

Population regions are based on where people live.

Name _____ Date _____

1 Test Preparation

Directions Read each question and choose the best answer. Then fill in the circle for the answer you have chosen. Be sure to fill in the circle completely.

1 What natural region is located at or near the foot of a mountain?
- Ⓐ peak
- Ⓑ hill
- Ⓒ piedmont
- Ⓓ humidity

2 Which of these is **not** the name of a landform?
- Ⓕ plain
- Ⓖ climate
- Ⓗ mountain
- Ⓙ valley

3 Which of these cause ocean currents?
- Ⓐ location
- Ⓑ elevation
- Ⓒ precipitation
- Ⓓ wind

4 Places in the rain shadow of a mountain receive very little—
- Ⓕ sunlight.
- Ⓖ precipitation.
- Ⓗ wind.
- Ⓙ temperature.

5 Another name for *grassland* is—
- Ⓐ prairie.
- Ⓑ mesquite.
- Ⓒ lichens.
- Ⓓ tundra.

Use after reading Chapter 1, pages 16–53.

© Harcourt

The First to Arrive

Directions Read the list of statements below about the arrival of ancient peoples in the Americas. In the spaces provided, write *LB* if a statement refers to the land bridge theory, *EA* if it refers to the early-arrival theory, or *O* if it refers to origin theory.

1 __O__ The Blackfoot people tell a story of Old Man the Creator.

2 __LB__ Some scientists believe that between 12,000 and 40,000 years ago, Asian hunting groups reached present-day Alaska.

3 __EA__ Recent discoveries support the idea that ancient peoples came by boat to the Americas.

4 __EA__ Archaeologists in Brazil have discovered artifacts that may be 30,000 years old.

5 __O__ According to the Hurons, land was formed from soil found in a turtle's claws.

6 __O__ There are many people today who believe that the first Americans did not come from Asia or anywhere else.

7 __LB__ Following a path between glaciers, hunters slowly made their way farther into the Americas.

8 __EA__ At Meadowcroft Rock Shelter archaeologists discovered a few artifacts that are more than 19,000 years old.

9 __O__ Many present-day Native Americans believe that their people have always lived in the Americas.

10 __LB__ After thousands of years, Asian hunters reached what is today Alaska.

11 __EA__ In Monte Verde, Chile, archaeologists uncovered artifacts, animal bones, and a child's foot print that had been there for at least 13,000 years.

12 __LB__ At several different times the level of the oceans dropped causing dry land to appear between Asia and North America.

Name _____ Date _____

CHART AND GRAPH SKILLS
Read Time Lines

Directions The time line on this page lists events that happened in the Americas. Study the time line and then answer the questions below.

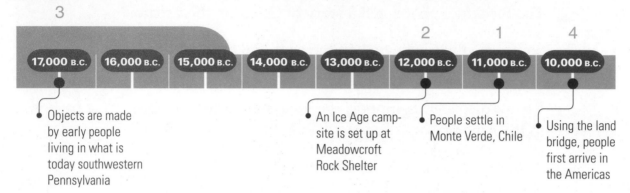

3

| 17,000 B.C. | 16,000 B.C. | 15,000 B.C. | 14,000 B.C. | 13,000 B.C. | 12,000 B.C. | 11,000 B.C. | 10,000 B.C. |

2   1   4

Objects are made by early people living in what is today southwestern Pennsylvania

An Ice Age camp-site is set up at Meadowcroft Rock Shelter

People settle in Monte Verde, Chile

Using the land bridge, people first arrive in the Americas

1 Artifacts found in Monte Verde, Chile, provide proof that people were there as

long ago as 11,000 B.C. _____.

2 Artifacts found at the Meadowcroft Rock Shelter suggest that people were

living there in 12,000 B.C. _____.

3 The oldest objects found at Meadowcroft Rock Shelter date back to

17,000 B.C. _____.

4 The land-bridge theory says people first arrived in the Americas around

10,000 B.C. _____.

Use after reading Chapter 2, Skill Lesson, pages 60–61.

© Harcourt

Ancient Indians

Directions Use the Word Bank below to complete a paragraph about the different cultures of the Olmecs, Maya, Mound Builders, and Anasazi.

technology	nomads	Mound Builders	agriculture	civilization	extinct
Anasazi	classes	slaves	pueblos	tribes	

The Olmec _____civilization_____ lived in what is now southeastern Mexico. Because the Olmecs remained in one place, they were not

considered _____nomads_____ . The Olmecs shared their ideas with

other cultures, or _____tribes_____ , such as the Maya. The Olmecs

and Maya were divided into separate social _____classes_____ , based upon people's occupations. At the bottom of Mayan society were

_____slaves_____ , or people forced to work against their will. At about the same time, a group of Native Americans began building a society in what is today the southeastern United States. These people were known as

_____Mound Builders_____ because of the earthen mounds they built as places of burial or worship. Hundreds of years later, a group called the

_____Anasazi_____ built a society in what is today the southwestern United States. In this society, people lived in groups of houses built closely

together. These houses were called _____pueblos_____ , the Spanish word for "village."

Name _____ Date _____

MAP AND GLOBE SKILLS
Use a Cultural Map

Directions Use the map to
answer the following questions.

1 According to the map, Native
Americans of the Desert Southwest
lived in parts of which present-day

states? Arizona and New Mexico
_____

2 What generalization can you make
about the location of settlements in
the Desert Southwest?

Settlements were spread fairly

evenly across the present-day

states of Arizona and New Mexico

and usually were located near

water.

3 Why do you think the Navajos
learned certain customs from the
Hopis rather than from the Pima?

The Navajos lived closer to the Hopis than they did to the Pimas.

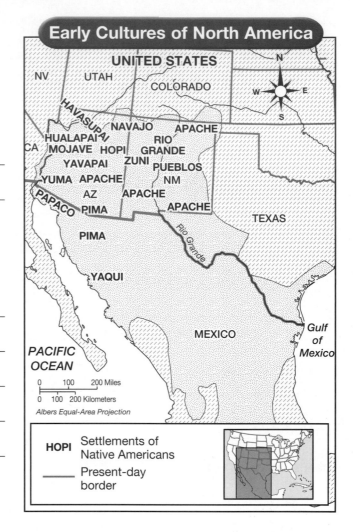

4 What generalization can you make about the ways of life of Native Americans

who lived in the Southwest? To cope with desert heat and little rainfall,

the people built their homes near a source of water they could use

to irrigate their crops.

The Desert Southwest

Directions On the blanks provided, write the word or name that best completes each sentence. Some letters in your answers will have numbers underneath them. Write these letters on the numbered blanks below, and you will find the name of a region in the United States.

1 Many Native Americans who lived in the __d__ __e__ __s__ __e__ __r__ __t__
                                                      1

were able to change the way they lived and adjust to the land and its resources.

2 Native American tribes such as the Hopis and

Zunis lived in __p__ __u__ __e__ __b__ __l__ __o__ __s__ .
                                            2

3 They learned that by growing a __s__ __u__ __r__ __p__ __l__ __u__ __s__ of food
                                                    3
they could survive during times of harsh weather.

4 Many of the crops grown by Native Americans were

__s__ __t__ __a__ __p__ __l__ __e__ foods such as corn, beans, and squash.
        4

5 The Hopis worshiped many gods and spirits, including

__k__ __a__ __c__ __h__ __i__ __n__ __a__ __s__ , who were believed to visit
                        5
their world once a year.

6 Around the year 1025, the Hopis were joined on their lands by

__n__ __e__ __w__ __c__ __o__ __m__ __e__ __r__ __s__ , such as the Navajos.
                6

7 The Navajos settled in an area known as the __F__ __o__ __u__ __r__

__C__ __o__ __r__ __n__ __e__ __r__ __s__ region, where parts of present-day
                        7
Arizona, Colorado, New Mexico, and Utah meet.

8 The Navajos learned many customs from the Hopis, including how to build

dome-shaped shelters called __h__ __o__ __g__ __a__ __n__ __s__ .
                                                        8

9 The Navajos' use of Hopi ways was an example of their ability to

__a__ __d__ __a__ __p__ __t__ to desert life.
                        9

__s__	__o__	__u__	__t__	__h__	__w__	__e__	__s__	__t__
1	2	3	4	5	6	7	8	9

© Harcourt

Name _____ Date _____

The Northwest Coast and the Arctic

Directions Complete the following chart by comparing and contrasting the ways of life of the Northwest Coast and Arctic Indians, and then answer the questions that follow.

Northwest Coast Indians	Arctic Indians
lived in a land of rivers and forests	lived in a land of snow and ice
lived in wooden houses	lived in igloos, tents, and huts
had many resources	had few resources
hunted salmon, other fish, and whales	hunted whales, seals, walrus, caribou
used trees to build shelter and make tools	used animal parts to build shelters and make tools

1 Contrast the living environments of the Northwest Coast and Arctic Indians.

The Northwest Coast Indians lived in a land of rivers and forests, while the

Arctic Indians lived in a land of snow and ice.

2 Describe the resources that the Northwest Coast and Arctic Indians used for

building shelters and making tools. The Northwest Coast Indians used trees to

build shelters and make tools, while the Arctic Indians used animal parts to build

shelters and make tools.

3 Using the information from the chart as a guide, write a paragraph comparing and contrasting the ways of life of the Northwest Coast and Arctic Indians.

The Northwest Coast Indians lived in a land of rivers and forests. The forests

provided wood to build houses and make tools. They hunted whales and fish,

such as salmon. In contrast, the Arctic Indians lived in a land of snow and ice

with few resources. They lived in igloos, tents, and huts and used animal parts to

make shelter and tools. Like the Northwest Coast Indians, the Arctic Indians

hunted whales in addition to seal, walrus, and caribou.

Use after reading Chapter 2, Lesson 4, pages 76–80.

Name _____   Date _____

The Plains

Directions Match the items below to the buffalo parts from which they were made. You will use some parts more than once. Then answer the questions.

A. hides

B. stomach

C. hair

D. bones and horns

E. meat

____A____ clothing

____B____ bags for water

____C____ cord

____D____ needles and tools

____A____ blankets

____E____ fresh or dried food

____A____ moccasins

____A____ tepee coverings

1 Of the parts listed above, which was used for the most purposes?

hides

2 What parts would the Plains Indians have used to make their shelters?

hides, bones and horns, and hair

3 What buffalo part do you think was most useful? Student responses will vary

but may indicate that meat was most important because of the need for food.

_____

© Harcourt

The Eastern Woodlands

Directions Read the paragraph. Then answer the questions that follow.

In the late 1500s, Iroquois villages often battled among themselves. Often, these battles grew out of small disputes that led to ill will between villages. According to tradition, a Huron named Deganawida believed that the battles must stop if the Iroquois tribes were to protect their ways of life from European newcomers. Deganawida persuaded a Mohawk leader named Hiawatha to join him in spreading the message throughout Iroquois country that "All shall receive the Great Law and labor together for the welfare of man."

The result of their effort was a confederation called the Iroquois League, made up of the Five Nations of the Seneca, the Cayuga, the Onondaga, the Oneida, and the Mohawk. A few years later a sixth nation, the Tuscarora, joined the confederacy.

Each nation in the league governed itself, and matters often were settled by unanimous vote. Very important matters, such as war, were left for discussion by a Great Council of 50 chiefs.

1 Who was Deganawida? According to tradition, he was a Huron who, with a Mohawk named Hiawatha, convinced the Iroquois tribes that they must stop their battles and work together to protect their ways of life.

2 What tribes belonged to the Iroquois League? the Seneca, the Cayuga, the Onondaga, the Oneida, the Mohawk, and later, the Tuscarora

3 How were decisions made by the Iroquois League? Each nation governed itself, but important issues, such as war, were decided by a Great Council of 50 chiefs.

4 What do you think Deganawida meant when he said "All shall receive the Great Law and labor together for the welfare of man"? He meant that if the nations joined together and worked for the common good all Iroquois would benefit.

_____

© Harcourt

Name _____ Date _____

CITIZENSHIP SKILLS
Resolve Conflict

Directions Complete the graphic organizer below. For each step, write the decisions that led to the formation of the Iroquois League.

ALL SIDES CLEARLY STATE WANTS AND NEEDS

Answers should reflect that the Iroquois had competing wants and needs for resources such as land, which prevented them from achieving lasting peace among tribes.

ALL SIDES DECIDE WHAT IS MOST IMPORTANT

Answers should reflect that the Five Nations sided with Deganawida and

Hiawatha in believing that lasting peace was most important.

ALL SIDES PLAN AND DISCUSS POSSIBLE COMPROMISES

Accept all answers indicating that a new governing body would help resolve various disputes while working toward the common good. Without such a governing body, disputes likely would continue and lasting peace would not be achieved.

ALL SIDES PLAN A LASTING COMPROMISE

Answers should mention the formation and structure of the Iroquois League, particularly the power awarded to a Great Council to decide matters of great importance.

Indians of the Plains and Northwest Coast

Directions Complete this graphic organizer to compare and contrast the Indians of the Plains and the Indians of the Northwest Coast.

The Plains Indians   **The Northwest Coast Indians**

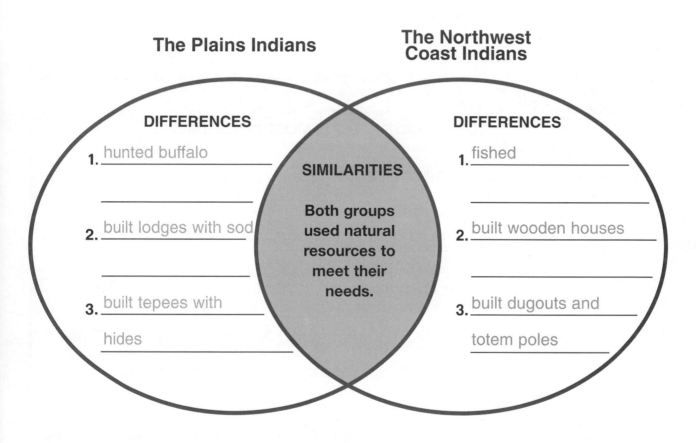

DIFFERENCES

1. hunted buffalo _____

2. built lodges with sod _____

3. built tepees with _____

   hides _____

SIMILARITIES

Both groups used natural resources to meet their needs.

DIFFERENCES

1. fished _____

2. built wooden houses _____

3. built dugouts and _____

   totem poles _____

© Harcourt

Name _____ Date _____

2 Test Preparation

Directions Read each question and choose the best answer. Then fill in the circle for the answer you have chosen. Be sure to fill in the circle completely.

1 Which of the following explains early settlement in the Americas?
Ⓐ land-bridge theory
Ⓑ early-arrival theory
Ⓒ origin stories
Ⓓ all of the above

2 Which of the following shows the correct order of the development of civilizations in the Americas?
Ⓕ the Olmecs, the Maya, the Mound Builders, the Anasazi
Ⓖ the Olmecs, the Mound Builders, the Maya, the Anasazi
Ⓗ the Maya, the Olmecs, the Mound Builders, the Anasazi
Ⓙ the Olmecs, the Maya, the Anasazi, the Mound Builders

3 Which statement **best** describes the people of the Desert Southwest?
Ⓐ They adapted their ways of life to fit their environment.
Ⓑ They believed in gods of the sun, rain, and Earth.
Ⓒ They lived in dome-shaped shelters called hogans.
Ⓓ They shared certain customs.

4 Unlike the Northwest Coast Indians, the Arctic Indians—
Ⓕ used animals for most of their food, shelter, and tools.
Ⓖ lived in villages.
Ⓗ hunted whales.
Ⓙ raised their food on farms.

5 The Iroquois League—
Ⓐ was a confederation made up of the Five Nations.
Ⓑ relied on a Great Council to make important decisions.
Ⓒ put an end to most Iroquois fighting.
Ⓓ all of the above.

© Harcourt

Use after reading Chapter 2, pages 54–93.

The Land of North America

Directions Study the names in the box below. Then use them to complete the sentences.

Appalachian Mountains	St. Lawrence Lowlands	fjords
Hudson Bay Lowlands	Río Bravo del Norte	Sierra Madre Occidental
Baja California	Interior Plains	Plateau of Mexico
Coast Mountains		

1 The _____Interior Plains_____ are a part of the Great Plains, which cover much of the United States and Canada.

2 The Rio Grande is known as the _____Río Bravo del Norte_____ in Mexico. This river forms much of the border between Mexico and the United States.

3 _____Baja California_____ is a long, narrow peninsula that lies northwest of the Mexican mainland.

4 Canada's smallest region has that country's greatest population. This region is the _____St. Lawrence Lowlands_____.

5 Among the _____Appalachian Mountains_____ in eastern Canada are valleys and lowland plains rich in forests.

6 Between the Plateau of Mexico and the Pacific Ocean is a mountain range called the _____Sierra Madre Occidental_____.

7 The _____Plateau of Mexico_____ rises to more than 8,000 feet (2,400 m) above sea level near Mexico City.

8 The _____Hudson Bay Lowlands_____ region is flat, and the land is poorly drained.

9 The _____Coast Mountains_____ form a cordillera along the western coast of Canada.

10 Canada's Arctic Islands region has deep, narrow inlets called _____fjords_____.

© Harcourt

Use after reading Unit 1, pages U1-1 to U1-15.

Name _____ Date _____

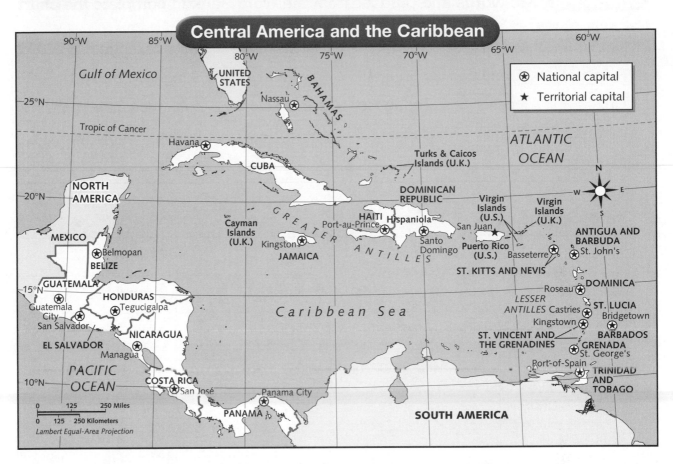

Central America and the Caribbean

11 ____T____ The southernmost end of Central America is the Isthmus of Panama.

_____

12 ____F____ The largest island in the Greater Antilles is Puerto Rico.

The largest island in the Greater Antilles is Cuba.

13 ____T____ To the west of Central America lies the Pacific.

_____

14 ____F____ Cuba, Jamaica, Hispaniola, and Grenada make up the Greater Antilles.

Cuba, Jamaica, Hispaniola, and Puerto Rico make up the Greater Antilles.

15 ____F____ The Republic of Haiti occupies the eastern two-thirds of Hispaniola.

The Republic of Haiti occupies the western one-third of Hispaniola.

Name _____   Date _____

The World in the 1400s

Directions Use words and phrases from the Word Bank to complete the chart.

Aztecs	Mali	Ghana	Renaissance	Lake Texcoco
Portugal	Timbuktu	quipus	Vijayanagar	Songhay Empire
Cuzco	Incas	Zheng He	carved ivory	Johannes Gutenberg
compass	China	Benin	the Bible	Andes Mountains
junks				

The Americas	Europe	Asia	Africa
Aztecs	the Bible	junks	Ghana
Incas	Portugal	China	Timbuktu
Cuzco	Renaissance	Zheng He	Mali
quipus	Johannes Gutenberg	Vijayanagar	Songhay Empire
Andes Mountains		compass	Benin
Lake Texcoco			carved ivory

Directions Write your answer to each question.

1 In what ways did the peoples of the Americas, Europe, Asia, and Africa interact with one another in the 1400s? The peoples of these lands interacted by exploration and trade.

2 How did China change after the death of its ruler Yong Le?
Yong Le encouraged exploration of other lands; the new rulers decided to stop all voyages and keep China apart from other civilizations.

Use after reading Chapter 3, Lesson 1, pages 106–111.

© Harcourt

Name _____   Date _____

MAP AND GLOBE SKILLS

Follow Routes on a Map

The Chinese Emperor sent admiral Zheng He, an explorer, on several voyages to explore the oceans surrounding China. From 1405 to 1433, Zheng He's fleets sailed on at least seven voyages. The admiral and his crew used wooden sailing ships called junks. The junks had flat bottoms, high masts, and square sails. Zheng He's expeditions took him to trading centers along the coast of China, as well as to the cities of Majapahit, Calicut, Hormuz, Mecca, and Mogadishu.

Directions **Use the map to help you answer the questions.**

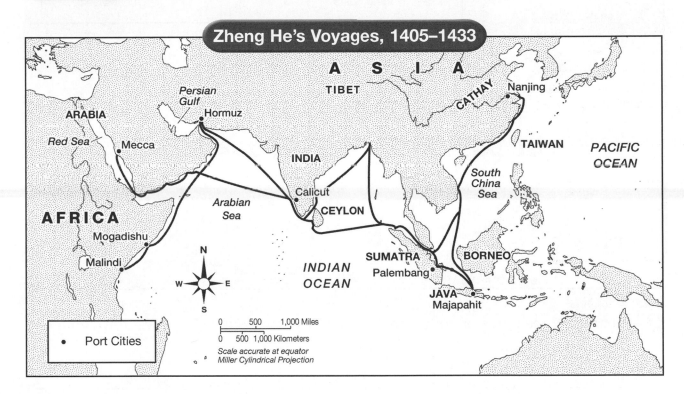

1 In what country is Calicut located? <u>India</u>

2 Zheng He started his voyages in Cathay, or China. In which directions did he travel to reach Hormuz? <u>south, then northwest</u>

3 In what direction did Zheng He travel to get from Hormuz to Mogadishu?

<u>southwest</u>

4 What city in Arabia did Zheng He visit? <u>Mecca</u>

Use after reading Chapter 3, Skill Lesson, pages 112–113.

Activity Book ▪ **27**

© Harcourt

Background to European Exploration

Name _____ Date _____

Directions Use the map and key to help you answer the questions. Write your answers in the blanks provided.

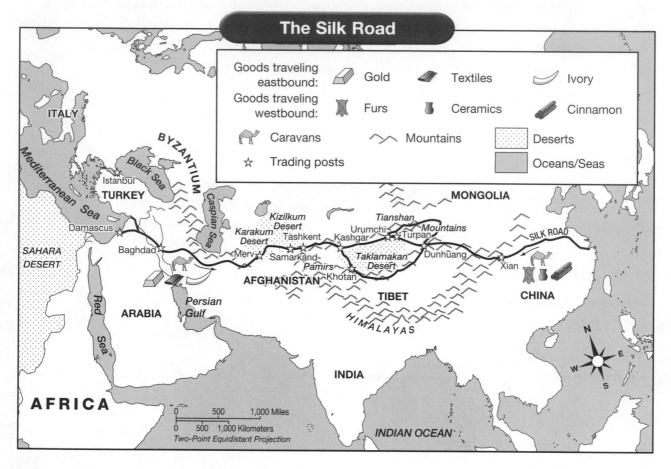

The Silk Road

Goods traveling eastbound:
- Gold
- Textiles
- Ivory

Goods traveling westbound:
- Furs
- Ceramics
- Cinnamon

- Caravans
- Mountains
- Deserts
- Trading posts
- Oceans/Seas

1 What are three kinds of goods transported by caravans traveling west through the Taklamakan Desert?

_____furs_____ , _____ceramics_____ , _____cinnamon_____

2 What three kinds of terrain would a caravan cross when traveling from Istanbul to Xian?

_____water_____ , _____mountains_____ , _____desert_____

3 What three deserts are along the Silk Road?

_____Kizilkum_____ , _____Taklamakan_____ , _____Karakum_____

Use after reading Chapter 3, Lesson 2, pages 114–119.

© Harcourt

Name _____ Date _____

READING SKILLS
Identify Causes and Their Effects

Directions Write the cause for each effect in the box provided.

Emperor Sunni Aui comes to power	development of the astrolabe	development of the caravel
invention of the compass	Turks capture Constantinople	cartographers begin working together
expeditions	Silk Road	

The compass—ancient and modern

CAUSE	→	EFFECT
expeditions		enabled explorers to discover new lands and established routes for future explorations
Turks capture Constantinople		closed the Silk Road, stopping trade between Europe and Asia
development of the caravel		enabled explorers and merchants to travel long distances at a faster speed while carrying more cargo; led to more extended ocean exploration
invention of the compass		navigational tool that allowed longer voyages and more accurate sailing
Silk Road		enabled Europeans to travel over land to Asian trade cities
cartographers begin working together		improved navigation by making more accurate maps
development of the astrolabe		improved navigation by helping sailors use the position of the sun or the North Star to find their location

© Harcourt

Use after reading Chapter 3, Skill Lesson, page 120.

Name _____   Date _____

Europeans Reach the Americas

Columbus

Directions Complete the chart using the information in the Word Bank. **Some pieces of information may be used more than once.**

Home Country	Planned Destination	Expedition Date	Importance of Exploration
Italy	Asia	1497	He was the first explorer to prove Vespucci's idea.
Portugal	Cathay	1499	The king of England sent him to find great riches.
Spain	The Isthmus of Panama	1500	He claimed Brazil for Portugal.
		1513	He realized that he and other explorers had found an unknown continent.
		1522	His attempt to find a western route to Asia led the Europeans to the Americas.

Explorer	Home Country	Planned Destination	Expedition Date	Importance of Exploration
Columbus	Italy	Asia	1492	His attempt to find a western route to Asia led the Europeans to the Americas.
Caboto	Italy	Cathay	1497	The king of England sent him to find great riches.
Magellan	Spain	Asia	1522	He was the first explorer to sail around the world.
Vespucci	Italy	Asia	1499	He realized that he and other explorers had found an unknown continent.
Balboa	Spain	The Isthmus of Panama	1513	He was the first explorer to prove Vespucci's idea.
Cabral	Portugal	Brazil	1500	He claimed Brazil for Portugal.

Use after reading Chapter 3, Lesson 3, pages 121–126.

The Spanish Conquerors

Ponce de León

Directions Write "T" or "F" in the blank before each statement to tell whether it is TRUE or FALSE. If the statement is FALSE, write the word that would make it TRUE in the blank at the end of the statement.

___F___ **1** The <u>English</u> king offered grants of money to explorers who would lead expeditions. <u>Spanish</u>

___T___ **2** In 1513 Ponce de León set out to find <u>Bimini</u> and the "Fountain of Youth." _____

___F___ **3** Ponce de León claimed the land now known as Florida and named it *La Florida*, which is Spanish for "conquer." <u>"flowery"</u>

___F___ **4** Cortés had heard stories about the great wealth of the <u>Inca</u> Empire. <u>Aztec</u>

___T___ **5** In 1519 Cortés traveled from the tropical coast to the Valley of Mexico, finally reaching <u>Tenochtitlán</u>. _____

___F___ **6** The <u>French</u> who were unhappy with Aztec rule gave the Spanish food and support against the Aztecs. <u>Native Americans</u>

___T___ **7** The Aztec people believed that Cortés might be <u>Quetzalcoatl</u>. _____

___F___ **8** The survivors of Narváez's expedition sailed along the <u>Pacific Coast</u> until they reached Spanish lands in Mexico. <u>Gulf Coast</u>

___F___ **9** Coronado and several Spaniards, Africans, and Native Americans set out to find the Seven Cities of <u>Steel</u>. <u>Gold</u>

___F___ **10** In 1539 Hernando de Soto explored much of the North American <u>Northwest</u>. <u>Southeast</u>

© Harcourt

Use after reading Chapter 3, Lesson 4, pages 127–133.

Name _____ Date _____

Search for the Northwest Passage

Directions Use the Word Bank below to complete the sentences.

Arctic Ocean	Northwest Passage	estuary	*Half Moon*
gold	Iroquois	Dutch East India Company	*Dauphine*
King Francis I	Staten Island		Pamlico Sound

1 European explorers were looking for the _____Northwest Passage_____,
a waterway along the north coast of North America connecting
the Atlantic Ocean and the Pacific Ocean.

2 In 1524 Giovanni da Verrazano set sail for North America

on his ship, the _____*Dauphine*_____ .

Verrazano

3 A narrow body of water called the _____Pamlico Sound_____
lay between the Atlantic Ocean and what Verrazano thought was
the Pacific Ocean.

4 Verrazano landed on the north end of present-day

_____Staten Island_____ .

Cartier

5 _____King Francis I_____ sent Jacques Cartier

to North America to search for _____gold_____
and other valuable metals.

6 Cartier's ship sailed up the _____estuary_____
of the St. Lawrence River.

7 During his expedition, Cartier was told by the _____Iroquois_____
of jewels and metals that could be found northwest of Gaspe Peninsula.

8 Henry Hudson sailed by way of the _____Arctic Ocean_____
in search of the Northwest Passage.

9 The _____Dutch East India Company_____ gave Hudson
a ship for his third voyage, his last attempt to find the
Northwest Passage.

Hudson

10 Hudson's crew aboard the _____*Half Moon*_____
mutinied in 1609.

Use after reading Chapter 3, Lesson 5, pages 136–139.

© Harcourt

European Exploration

Directions Complete this graphic organizer to show that you understand the causes and effects of some of the key events that encouraged exploration and led to the discovery of the Americas.

CAUSE	EFFECT	EFFECT
Columbus gets King Ferdinand and Queen Isabella to support his expedition.	Columbus is able to sail west with 89 sailors and three ships.	Columbus lands at San Salvador.

CAUSE	EFFECT	EFFECT
De Soto and an army of 600 soldiers sail to the west coast of Florida in search of gold.	In their unsuccessful three-year search for gold, de Soto and his army explore all of what is today the southeastern United States.	The Spanish claim all of what is today the southeastern United States.

3 Test Preparation

Directions Read each question and choose the best answer. Then fill in the circle for the answer you have chosen. Be sure to fill in the circle completely.

1 Many years before Europeans arrived in the Americas, some groups of Native Americans had established powerful—
- Ⓐ tribes.
- Ⓑ fleets of ships.
- Ⓒ empires.
- Ⓓ trade agreements with China.

2 A compass and an astrolabe are kinds of _____ sailors used to determine their location at sea.
- Ⓕ construction tools
- Ⓖ navigational tools
- Ⓗ books
- Ⓙ telescopes

3 When Columbus landed in the Americas, he thought he was in _____.
- Ⓐ Asia
- Ⓑ Spain
- Ⓒ Mexico
- Ⓓ Portugal

4 The Portuguese explorer _____ was the first to sail around the world.
- Ⓕ Columbus
- Ⓖ Magellan
- Ⓗ Vespucci
- Ⓙ Cabral

5 King Francis I was one of many European rulers who wanted to find the _____ through North America.
- Ⓐ Santa Fe Trail
- Ⓑ Silk Road
- Ⓒ trade route
- Ⓓ Northwest Passage

© Harcourt

New Spain

Directions Write the number of the sentence under the appropriate heading in the Venn diagram.

Before Spanish Colonies Established
3, 7, 8

Before and After
4, 9

After Spanish Colonies Established
1, 2, 5, 6, 10

1 Many Native Americans died from a disease called smallpox.

2 The Plains Indians tamed horses and used them for hunting.

3 Native Americans were free from European diseases.

4 Gold, silver, and other treasures could be found in North America.

5 Native American tribes living in the borderlands traded with the Spanish.

6 The Navajos raised sheep and wove the wool into colorful clothing and blankets.

7 People could not travel on the *El Camino Real.*

8 Many Native Americans lived as free peoples in what is today known as Mexico.

9 Many Native Americans followed their traditional religions.

10 Missionaries persuaded some Native Americans to become Catholics.

Use after reading Chapter 4, Lesson 1, pages 144–149.

© Harcourt

New France

Directions Fill in the missing information in this letter from a member of Louis Joliet's crew. Use the words below to help you complete the letter.

Jacques Marquette	Lake Michigan	Indian	canoes	1673
Northwest Passage	Mississippi	Spanish	languages	south

Dear Family:

In this year of _____1673_____, I think of you often. I have set out with Joliet's crew on an expedition to find a great river called the _____Mississippi_____. We are traveling with a missionary named _____Jacques Marquette_____ who speaks many Indian _____languages_____.

We started our journey from northern _____Lake Michigan_____ in birch-bark _____canoes_____. We crossed a huge lake and several rivers. At last we saw the great Mississippi! Unfortunately, we realized it was not the _____Northwest Passage_____ that we were looking for because it flows _____south_____.

When we reached the mouth of the Arkansas River, we met some _____Indian_____ people who told us of Europeans living farther south along the river. We think those Europeans might be the _____Spanish_____. We fear they may attack us, so we have decided to turn back.

I will think of you all as I journey home.

Sincerely,
François

Use after reading Chapter 4, Lesson 2, pages 150–155.

© Harcourt

The English in the Americas

Directions Some of these sentences are causes, and some are effects. Complete the chart to show each cause and its effect.

> "Sea dogs" like Francis Drake become pirates.
>
> Treasure captured by "sea dogs" helps increase England's wealth.
>
> England decides to start colonies in America.
>
> The English colonists at Roanoke Island arrive too late in the year to plant crops.

 CAUSE ➡ **EFFECT**

CAUSE	EFFECT
Elizabeth I encourages English sea captains to attack Spanish treasure ships.	"Sea dogs" like Francis Drake become pirates.
Treasure captured by "sea dogs" helps increase England's wealth.	England builds a strong navy with that wealth and becomes a powerful country.
Europe's most powerful countries have colonies in America.	England decides to start colonies in America.
The English colonists at Roanoke Island arrive too late in the year to plant crops.	John White returns to England to gather food and supplies.

Use after reading Chapter 4, Lesson 3, pages 156–159.

The Jamestown Colony

Directions Use the chart below to answer the questions that follow.

House of Burgesses			
Who?	**What?**	**When or Where?**	**How?**
Each Virginia settlement or plantation was allowed to elect two burgesses, usually wealthy landowners.	Virginia's legislature, the branch of the government that makes laws	Established July 30, 1619	Burgesses would meet once a year with the royal governor.
The 22 original burgesses were members of the House of Burgesses.	The first lawmaking assembly formed in the English colonies	Jamestown Colony	Burgesses and royal governor would meet to make local laws and decide on taxes.
Royal Governor George Yeardley shared ruling authority with the House of Burgesses.	Jamestown Colony would live under English law and have the same rights as the people living in England.	Met in the Jamestown church	Modeled after the English Parliament

1 What did the House of Burgesses do? They made laws for the Virginia Colony.

_____

2 What country ruled Jamestown? England _____

3 Who was the royal governor? George Yeardley _____

4 How often did the royal governor meet with the burgesses?

once a year _____

5 What governing body was the House of Burgesses modeled after?

the English Parliament _____

6 When was the House of Burgesses established? July 30, 1619 _____

7 How did the burgesses decide on laws and taxes? They met with the royal

governor. _____

8 How many burgesses could be elected from each plantation or settlement?

2 _____

Use after reading Chapter 4, Lesson 4, pages 160–164.

© Harcourt

Name _____ Date _____

CITIZENSHIP SKILLS
Solve a Problem

Directions One problem in colonial times was that of getting settlers to stay for long periods of time. Imagine that you are a leader who wants to settle a colony. Use the steps below to complete the boxes and help you solve the problem. Step 1 has been done for you.

Here are some questions to think about when solving your problem:

Where will the colonists live? How will they get food? How will they make a living? How will they prepare for winter? Who will govern the settlements? How will they respond to conflicts with other people?

Step 1
Identify the problem.

People are not

permanently settling

in the colonies.

Step 2
Gather information about the problem.

Step 2 should include reasons that colonists are not remaining, such as illness, starvation, conflicts with Native Americans, poor farming, not enough supplies.

Step 3
Think of and list possible options.

Step 3 should include ways to meet these challenges, such as moving to areas that offer better farming, training people to farm the land, storing enough food to get them through the winter.

Step 4
Consider the advantages and disadvantages of possible options.

Step 4 should offer advantages and disadvantages for each option: example—another area is better for farming but is occupied by Native Americans.

Step 5
Choose the best solution.

Step 5 should name the solution the student chooses to fix the problem, for example, teach colonists to survive with the skills they have.

Step 6
Try your solution.

Step 6 should explain how the solution would be applied to the problem.

Step 7
Think about how well your solution helps solve the problem.

Step 7 should list how the plan could work and reasons why it might not work.

© Harcourt

Use after reading Chapter 4, Skill Lesson, page 165.

The Plymouth Colony

Directions When the Mayflower Compact was written in 1620, the English language was very different from what it is today. Below is a version of the Mayflower Compact written in present-day language. Use it to answer the questions that follow.

The Mayflower Compact

In the name of God, Amen. We, the loyal subjects of King James and the people of God have taken a voyage to settle in the first colony in the northern parts of Virginia. We, the people whose names are signed below, have made an agreement, in the presence of God and one another, to establish our own government of fair and equal laws. These laws will be decided by the majority rule of this group. These laws are made for the good of the people in the colony as well as for the colony itself. We promise to obey the laws we have made. We have signed our names below, at Cape Cod, on November 11, 1620.

Myles Standish   *William Bradford*

1 Who is the English ruler named in the Mayflower Compact?

King James

2 Where did the Mayflower passengers think they were going to settle?

the northern parts of Virginia

3 How did the writers of the Mayflower Compact say laws would be decided?

They would be decided by majority rule.

4 What did the passengers promise? 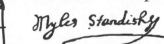 to obey the laws they made

5 Where and when was the Mayflower Compact signed? _____

Cape Cod; November 11, 1620

Use after reading Chapter 4, Lesson 5, pages 166–170.

© Harcourt

Name _____ Date _____

CHART AND GRAPH SKILLS

Compare Tables to Classify Information

Directions Read and study each table. Use the information in the tables to answer the questions below.

Table A: Native Americans and European Colonists		
Colony	**Native American Tribe Encountered**	**Interaction/Events**
Connecticut (1636)	Pequot	Colonists purchased land; later, tribe fought to reclaim land.
New Jersey (1664)	Lenape	Colonists fought with this hostile tribe.
New York (1626)	Algonquian-speaking tribes	Colonists bought Manhattan Island from local tribes.
Rhode Island (1636)	Algonquian-speaking tribes, mostly Narragansett	Colonists peacefully coexisted with local tribes.

Table B: Native Americans and European Colonists		
Interaction/Events	**Native American Tribe Encountered**	**Colony**
Colonists bought Manhattan Island from local tribes.	Algonquian-speaking tribes	New York (1626)
Colonists purchased land; later, tribe fought to reclaim land.	Pequot	Connecticut (1636)
Colonists peacefully coexisted with local tribes.	Algonquian-speaking tribes, mostly Narragansett	Rhode Island (1636)
Colonists fought with this hostile tribe.	Lenape	New Jersey (1664)

1 Which table makes it easier to find out when the first colony was established?

Why? Table B; the Colony column is in date order.

2 Which table would you use to find which colony bought an island from Native

Americans? Why? Table B; the interaction is in the first column.

3 Which table would you use to find out which Native American tribe was found

in New Jersey? Why? Table A; states listed are in the first column.

Use after reading Chapter 4, Skill Lesson, page 171.

Activity Book ■ 41

© Harcourt

Key Settlements in North America

Directions Complete this graphic organizer by categorizing people and settlements with the country they are associated with.

SPANISH SETTLEMENTS	FRENCH SETTLEMENTS	ENGLISH SETTLEMENTS
KEY PEOPLE	**KEY PEOPLE**	**KEY PEOPLE**
1. **Bartolomé de Las Casas**	1. **Samuel de Champlain**	1. **Sir Francis Drake**
2. Pedro Menéndez de Avilés	2. Count de Frontenac	2. Sir Walter Raleigh
3. Junípero Serra	3. Pierre LeMoyne/Jean Baptiste LeMoyne	3. John White
KEY SETTLEMENTS	**KEY SETTLEMENTS**	**KEY SETTLEMENTS**
1. **Hispaniola**	1. **Quebec**	1. **Roanoke**
2. Castillo de San Marcos	2. St. Louis, Des Moines	2. Jamestown
3. Nombre de Dios	3. New Orleans	3. Plymouth Colony

Name _____ Date _____

4 Test Preparation

Directions Read each question and choose the best answer. Then fill in the circle for the answer you have chosen. Be sure to fill in the circle completely.

1 What did the Spanish create in North America to protect their colonies from other Europeans?
  Ⓐ a hacienda
  Ⓑ a buffer zone
  Ⓒ a mission
  Ⓓ a ranch

2 What was the main item of trade between the French and the Native Americans in New France?
  Ⓕ fur
  Ⓖ gold
  Ⓗ silk
  Ⓙ food

3 Who protected the English "sea dogs" when they stole treasures from the Spanish?
  Ⓐ Native Americans
  Ⓑ the French
  Ⓒ the queen of England
  Ⓓ conquistadors

4 What is a burgess?
  Ⓕ a representative
  Ⓖ a royal governor
  Ⓗ a company
  Ⓙ a monarchy

5 Why did the Pilgrims sail to North America in 1620?
  Ⓐ to meet Native Americans
  Ⓑ to practice their religion in their own way
  Ⓒ to be farmers
  Ⓓ to trade fur

Use after reading Chapter 4, pages 144–171.

Name _____ Date _____

Further Encounters

Directions Many ethnic groups settled in Central America and the Caribbean. Read the descriptions below. Draw one or more lines connecting each description with the group or place it describes.

1 Scientists believe that this group was the first to settle in the Caribbean region.

2 These three groups lived in the Caribbean region during the 1300s and the 1400s.

3 These countries began settlements on the islands of the Caribbean in the early 1600s.

4 This group built more than 100 cities in what are today Belize, El Salvador, Guatemala, and Honduras.

5 This group forced the Arawaks to work as slaves on large plantations.

Arawaks

Ciboneys

Caribs

England

France

Netherlands

Maya

Spanish

Directions On a separate sheet of paper, write a paragraph that explains how colonists from the Netherlands, England, France, and Spain influenced the people who lived in the region. Responses should mention that Europeans conquered and enslaved people but also introduced new foods, new animals, and new ways of doing things.

© Harcourt

Name _____ Date _____

Group or Nation	Region of Canada	Natural Resources Used
Algonkins	St. Lawrence Lowlands	They used wood and tree bark for homes and canoes. They used rivers and lakes to help them trade with other groups.
Assiniboines	Interior Plains	They hunted bison, which they used for tools, weapons, and food and for making clothing and shelters.
Crees	Northern Canadian Shield	They relied on hunting small animals because the growing season was too short for farming.
Haidas	Western Canada	They used cedar trees to build shelters and canoes. They hunted for whales, sea otters, and other ocean animals.
Inuit	Arctic region	They made tools, weapons, and artwork from animals' bones, antlers, horns, and teeth. They used animal skins for tents and earth to build homes. They used snow and ice to build igloos.

Massachusetts Bay Colony

Directions Find the terms in the Word Bank in the Word Search Puzzle.
Words may be arranged vertically, horizontally, or diagonally.

Puritan	charter	common	specialize	town meeting
public office	blacksmith	churn	colony	confederation
school	constable	kettle	patchwork quilts	candles
livestock	soap	crops	preserved	pickled vegetables

```
y s d e h c s o o c v d c a n d l e s b q z s d f w q
h k o f d e s n a h r t e d f h j c c o l o n y u b t
n r v y q w p r e s e r v e d a o y k a n b m k g b
y t r d c t d e a m c b n t i u u d h p c p x v c s l
t j u u o r d c e t o w n m e e t i n g a u a k r f a
n m t l n o l u p i c k l e d v e g e t a b l e s q c
k g f t s e d t u y h h j k g o y t g b j l s f d a k
d e i b t u y t r c a x w l k u j h v y u i c z i x s
c r t v a b c n i l r v c o m m o n y a o c r m x u m
b t f t b j h k t v t x h d r l k i j d c o k s d s i
i u f r l h z s a r e g u g m k g h r f y f e r p c t
w s b n e e k m n y r e r s d e q j f w d f j o d h h
o l p u h j f r t d o k n f d e t u i u y i r x c o m
w d e s s p e c i a l i z e t f h y i r e c i u k o p
u e h s g a i w k e d j o l h j i k g l t e c w o l n
k l n f l i v e s t o c k d a s j w e h t a g n c b d
m f d j s e i c o n f e d e r a t i o n k s s a e l s
```

(continued)

© Harcourt

Name _____ Date _____

Directions Use words from the word bank on the previous page to complete the sentences below.

1. In 1628 King Charles I granted a _____ charter _____,
to a group of Puritans, allowing them to settle in New England.

2. John Winthrop served as governor in one _____ colony _____
several times during a 20-year period.

3. Winthrop formed a _____ confederation _____ among the people of
New England so they could better defend themselves against their enemies.

4. A place for the town animals to graze was one use for the
_____ common _____.

5. A _____ blacksmith _____ specialized in working with iron.

6. A law was passed stating that any town with more than 50 families must
have a _____ school _____.

7. Both men and women could attend a _____ town meeting _____,
but only the men could vote.

8. One public official was a _____ constable _____, who was in
charge of maintaining order and keeping the peace.

9. _____ Pickled vegetables _____ could be stored and eaten throughout
the winter.

10. Some food, as well as leather and wool, came from farmers'
_____ livestock _____.

Name _____ Date _____

New Ideas, New Colonies

Directions Complete the information in the boxes next to the map. Use the names and terms below to help you.

Thomas Hooker	Roger Williams	consent
John Endecott	Fundamental Orders	self-governed by Puritan leaders

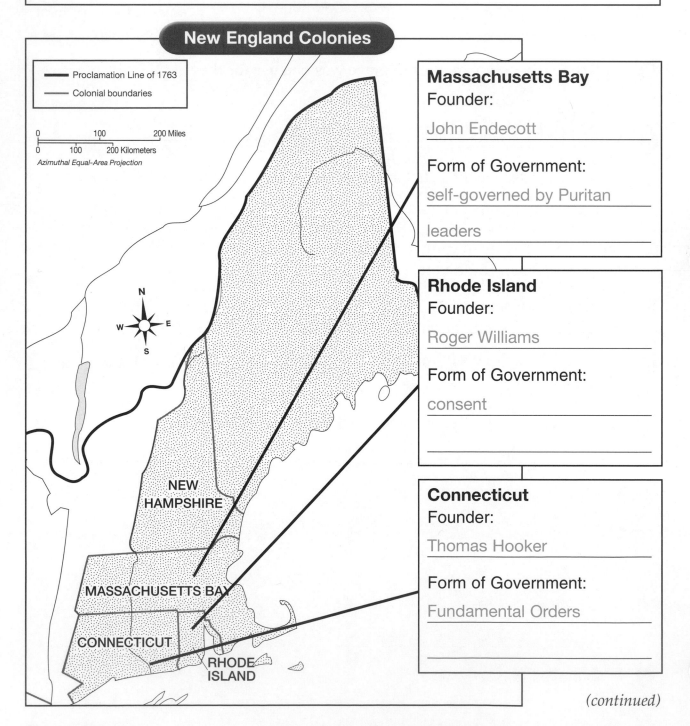

New England Colonies

Proclamation Line of 1763
Colonial boundaries

0   100   200 Miles
0   100   200 Kilometers
Azimuthal Equal-Area Projection

NEW HAMPSHIRE

MASSACHUSETTS BAY

CONNECTICUT

RHODE ISLAND

Massachusetts Bay
Founder:
John Endecott

Form of Government:
self-governed by Puritan
leaders

Rhode Island
Founder:
Roger Williams

Form of Government:
consent

Connecticut
Founder:
Thomas Hooker

Form of Government:
Fundamental Orders

(continued)

© Harcourt

Use after reading Chapter 5, Lesson 2, pages 194–199.

Name _____ Date _____

Directions Use the map on the previous page and the words and sentences below to help you complete the table and answer the questions.

Places, Tribes, and Dates:	Events:
1636 Narragansett Windsor, 1633 Providence, 1636	Expelled from the colony, Williams moved his family to Narragansett Bay. Puritans disagreed with practices of the Church of England.

Founded	Massachusetts Bay Colony	Rhode Island Colony	Connecticut Colony
When	1628	1636	1630s
Why	Puritans disagreed with practices of the Church of England.	Expelled from the colony, Williams moved his family to Narragansett Bay.	Some colonists were looking for better farmland; other colonists wanted religious freedom.
Where	Salem, 1628	Providence, 1636	Windsor, 1633
Which tribe was there?	Wampanoags	Narragansett	Pequots

1 When was the Connecticut Colony founded? _1630s_____

2 What was the major event that led to the founding of the Massachusetts Bay Colony? _Puritans disagreed with practices of the Church of England._____

3 What Native American tribe did the Massachusetts Bay Colony interact with?
_Wampanoags_____

4 Who moved to Narragansett Bay? _Roger Williams_____

Use after reading Chapter 5, Lesson 2, pages 194–199.

© Harcourt

New England's Economy

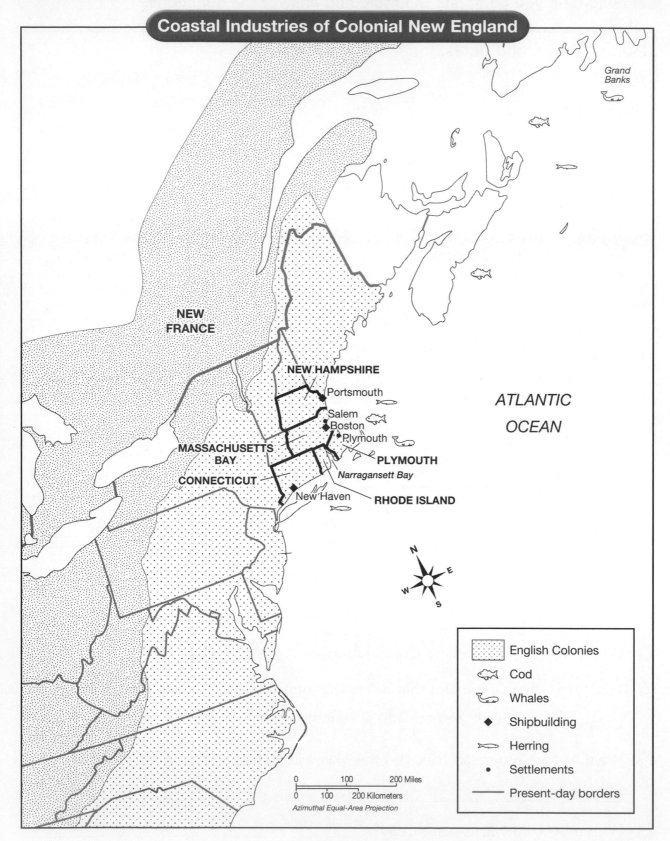

Coastal Industries of Colonial New England

Grand Banks

NEW
FRANCE

NEW HAMPSHIRE
Portsmouth

ATLANTIC

OCEAN

Salem
Boston
Plymouth

MASSACHUSETTS
BAY

PLYMOUTH

Narragansett Bay

CONNECTICUT

New Haven

RHODE ISLAND

	English Colonies
	Cod
	Whales
◆	Shipbuilding
	Herring
•	Settlements
—	Present-day borders

0   100   200 Miles
0   100   200 Kilometers
Azimuthal Equal-Area Projection

© Harcourt

(continued)

Name _____ Date _____

Directions Use the map on page 48 to help you answer some of the questions below.

1 Shade in the area that shows the New England Colonies.

2 Other than the English colonies, what land area was near the Grand Banks?

New France

3 In what three settlements and colonies were the shipbuilding centers located?

Portsmouth, New Hampshire; Boston, Massachusetts Bay; New Haven,

Connecticut

4 What were two locations where whales were caught? near Plymouth and in

the Grand Banks

5 In what ocean did the colonists fish? Atlantic Ocean

6 What important product came from whales, and what was it used for?

Whale fat, or blubber; it was used to make oil for lamps.

7 When whalers first began hunting, they used small rowboats and were able to find many whales near the shore. Later, the whalers needed bigger ships, and their whaling trips lasted much longer. Sometimes, whalers were gone for many months or even years. Explain why the whaling industry changed.

At first, there were many whales along the coast. Then, as more whalers

began hunting, the whale population decreased, so whalers had to travel

longer distances to find whales and were gone longer.

8 Why did shipbuilders choose coastal locations such as Portsmouth for

shipbuilding? They needed to be near the ocean to sail the ships and near

the forest to get the wood they needed. It was also much cheaper to

build ships in the colonies than to buy ships from England.

CHART AND GRAPH SKILLS
Use a Line Graph

Directions Study the line graph below. Use it to help you determine whether the statements on page 51 are true or false.

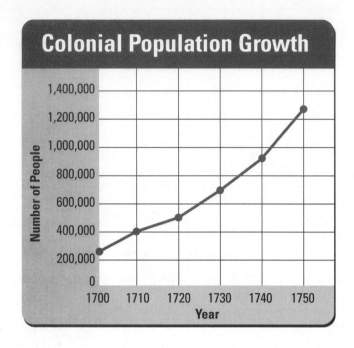

Colonial Population Growth

Directions Circle *T* if the sentence is true. Circle *F* if the sentence is false.

1 There were more than 2 million people in the colonies by 1750. T (F)

2 The population growth was less than 500,000 between 1700 and 1710. (T) F

3 There were nearly twice as many people in 1740 as there were in 1720. (T) F

4 One of the largest population increases occurred between 1720 and 1730. T (F)

(continued)

5 The population was almost a million people in 1740. ⓣ F

6 Given the growth of the population between 1740 and 1750, what would the projected population be for 1760? Read the graph, and list the numbers for each point on the graph.

1740 _about 920,000_____

1750 _about 1,250,000_____

1760 _about 1,580,000_____

7 By the early 1700s the colonies were well established and colonists were relatively healthy. Many colonists had large families—sometimes with ten or more children. In addition, new settlers continued to arrive. Using the line graph, explain the effect that these factors had on the population of the colonies.

_The population of the colonies continued to grow._____

_____

_____

© Harcourt

The Massachusetts Bay Colony

Directions Complete this graphic organizer by summarizing the following facts about the Massachusetts Bay Colony.

FACTS		SUMMARY

1. The Puritans built many villages in North America.

2. The most important building in a Puritan village was the meetinghouse.

3. The village meetinghouse served as a church and a place to hold town meetings.

In Puritan villages the most important building was the meetinghouse, which served as both a church and a place to hold town meetings.

---

1. Roger Williams was forced to leave the Massachusetts Bay Colony.

2. Anne Hutchinson was also forced to leave the colony.

3. Roger Williams and Anne Hutchinson and their followers established their own settlements.

Forced to leave the Massachusetts Bay Colony, both Roger Williams and Anne Hutchinson established their own settlements.

---

1. Trading goods made many people wealthy in New England.

2. Goods were traded between the colonies, England, and the west coast of Africa.

3. Trade brought the first African slaves to the English Colonies.

Though trade made many people in New England wealthy, it also brought the first African slaves to the English Colonies.

Name _____ Date _____

5 Test Preparation

Directions Read each question and choose the best answer. Then fill in the circle for the answer you have chosen. Be sure to fill in the circle completely.

1 Which group of people settled in New England because they disagreed with many practices of the Church of England?
- Ⓐ colonists
- Ⓑ settlers
- Ⓒ Puritans
- Ⓓ Christians

2 Who had a conflict with the Puritan leaders in the Massachusetts Bay Colony?
- Ⓕ Anne Hutchinson
- Ⓖ Roger Williams
- Ⓗ both F and G
- Ⓙ John Winthrop

3 Where did some colonists go to find better farmland?
- Ⓐ Rhode Island
- Ⓑ Connecticut
- Ⓒ Massachusetts Bay
- Ⓓ Plymouth

4 Why was whale oil a popular product?
- Ⓕ It burned brightly without an unpleasant odor.
- Ⓖ It was very inexpensive.
- Ⓗ It was available in unlimited quantities.
- Ⓙ both G and H

5 _____ were workers who used wood to make barrels and casks.
- Ⓐ Merchants
- Ⓑ Shipbuilders
- Ⓒ Fishermen
- Ⓓ Coopers

Use after reading Chapter 5, pages 188–205.

Breadbasket Colonies

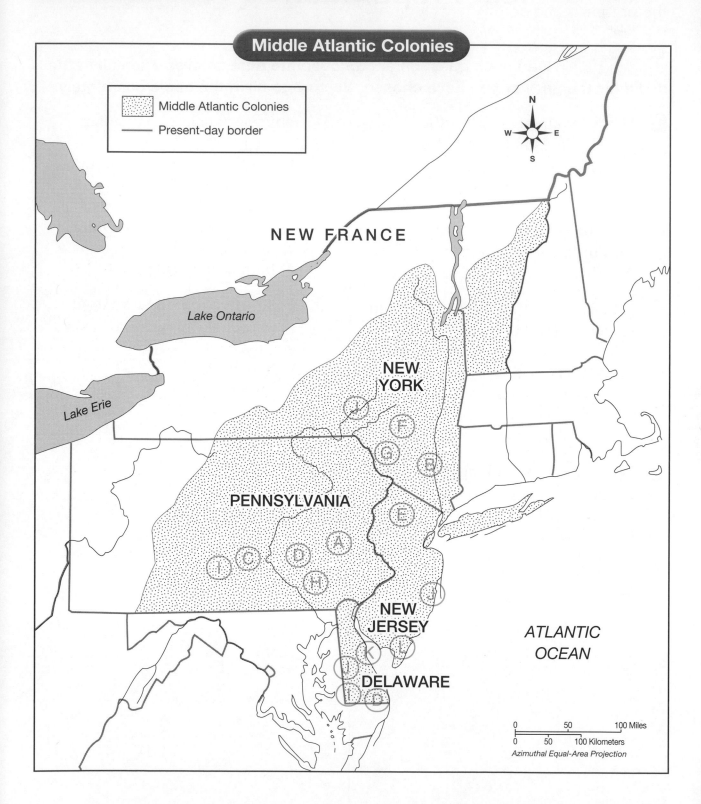

(continued)

Use after reading Chapter 6, Lesson 1, pages 210–215.

Name _____ Date _____

Directions Read each lettered phrase below. On the map, write the letter of the phrase in the colony or colonies to which it applies.

A. settled by Quakers Pennsylvania

B. bought from the Manhattan Indians by Peter Minuit New York

C. freedom of speech, freedom of worship, and trial by jury Pennsylvania

D. William Penn Pennsylvania and Delaware

E. John Berkeley and George Carteret New Jersey

F. colonists fought Delaware and Wappinger Indians New York

G. Peter Stuyvesant New York

H. "Penn's woods" Pennsylvania

I. Native American Chief Tamenend Pennsylvania and Delaware

J. claimed for Holland by Henry Hudson New York, New Jersey, and Delaware

K. Fort Christina Delaware

L. Edward Byllinge New Jersey

Why were the Middle Atlantic Colonies called the "breadbasket colonies"?

The Middle Atlantic Colonies were called the "breadbasket colonies" because they

produced many crops used in the making of bread, such as wheat, corn, and rye.

_____

_____

_____

_____

_____

_____

_____

© Harcourt

Colonial Philadelphia

Benjamin Franklin

William Penn

Facts About William Penn and Benjamin Franklin

Founded Philadelphia on the idea that people of different backgrounds could live in peace together

Wrote "Early to bed and early to rise makes a man healthy, wealthy, and wise"

Designed the layout of Philadelphia, with a "checkerboard" plan for the center

Printed a newspaper called the *Pennsylvania Gazette*

Organized the first firefighting company in the colonies

Named his colony's chief city Philadelphia

Worked to have Philadelphia's streets lit at night and paved

Divided his colony into townships made up of 5,000 acres each

Helped establish the first subscription library

Added public parks to the city he called "a green country town"

Planned the government and the settlements of Philadelphia

Invented the lightning rod, which helped protect buildings from lightning

(continued)

Name ______________________ Date ____________

Directions **Read the facts about William Penn and Benjamin Franklin on page 56. Decide which facts describe each person. Then use the facts to fill in the table below.**

William Penn	Benjamin Franklin
Named his colony's chief city Philadelphia	Organized the first firefighting company in the colonies
Planned the government and the settlements of Philadelphia	Worked to have Philadelphia's streets lit at night and paved
Added public parks to the city he called "a green country town"	Helped establish the first subscription library
Founded Philadelphia on the idea that people of different backgrounds could live in peace together	Invented the lightning rod, which helped protect buildings from lightning
Divided his colony into townships made up of 5,000 acres each	Printed a newspaper called the *Pennsylvania Gazette*
Designed the layout of Philadelphia, with a "checkerboard" plan for the center	Wrote "Early to bed and early to rise makes a man healthy, wealthy, and wise"

CHART AND GRAPH SKILLS

Use a Circle Graph

Directions Use the circle graph to help you answer the questions below.

Population of the 13 Colonies, 1750

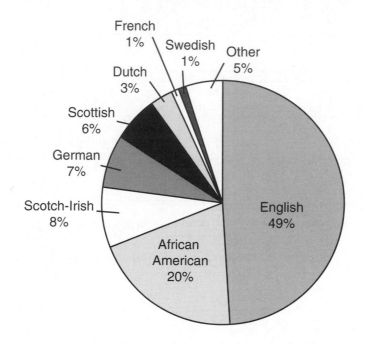

① What was the largest ethnic group in the 13 colonies in 1750?

English

② What were the smallest ethnic groups? Swedish and French

③ Which group was larger, German or Scottish? German

④ What percent of the population was African American? 20%

⑤ What was the combined percent of African American and English people?

69%

⑥ What was the combined percent of all non-English people?

51%

(continued)

© Harcourt

Name _____ Date _____

In addition to Quaker meetinghouses, there were many kinds of churches in Pennsylvania. Use the information in the table to make a circle graph of the kinds of churches in Pennsylvania other than Quaker meetinghouses.

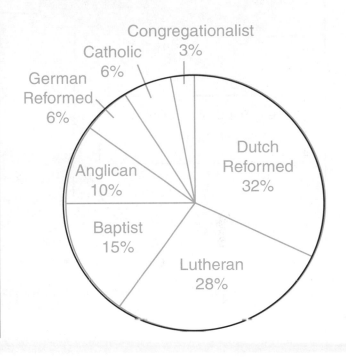

Pennsylvania Churches* in 1750	
Church	**Percent of Population**
Dutch Reformed	32%
Lutheran	28%
Baptist	15%
Anglican	10%
German Reformed	6%
Catholic	6%
Congregationalist	3%

*Quaker meetinghouses not included

Use the information from the circle graph you have made to write a paragraph about church memberships in Pennsylvania. Be sure to discuss why you think Pennsylvania had so many different kinds of churches.

Answers will vary but should mention how most people in Pennsylvania attended

Dutch Reform or Lutheran churches. Students should also mention that

Pennsylvania's religious diversity was a result of William Penn's idea that people

of different backgrounds and religions could live in peace together.

_____

_____

_____

_____

_____

© Harcourt

Use after reading Chapter 6, Skill Lesson, page 223.

Moving West

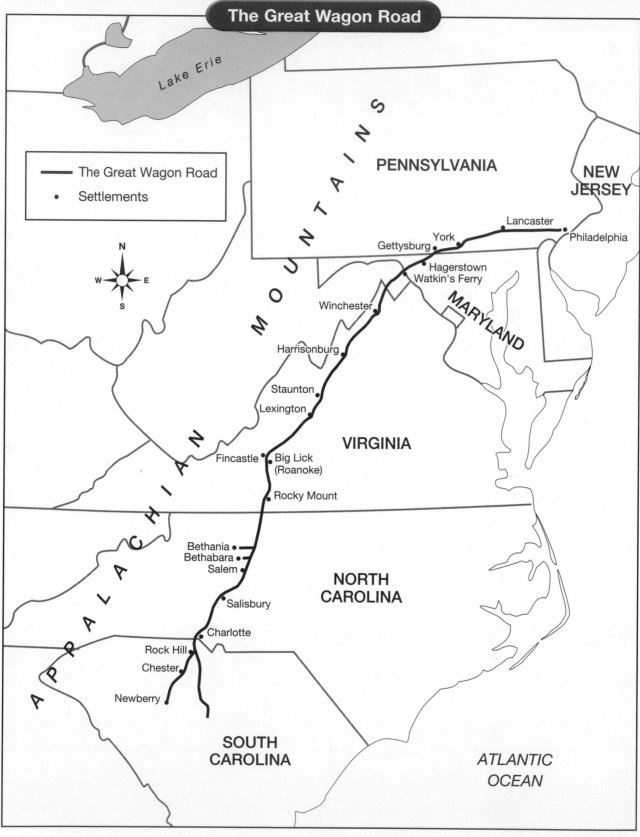

The Great Wagon Road

Lake Erie

— The Great Wagon Road
• Settlements

N W E S

PENNSYLVANIA

NEW JERSEY

M O U N T A I N S

Lancaster
York
Gettysburg
Philadelphia
Hagerstown
Watkin's Ferry

Winchester

MARYLAND

Harrisonburg

Staunton
Lexington

A P P A L A C H I A N

VIRGINIA

Fincastle • Big Lick
(Roanoke)

Rocky Mount

Bethania •
Bethabara •
Salem •

NORTH CAROLINA

• Salisbury

• Charlotte
Rock Hill •
Chester •

Newberry •

SOUTH CAROLINA

ATLANTIC OCEAN

© Harcourt

(continued)

Use after reading Chapter 6, Lesson 3, pages 224–227.

Name _____ Date _____

Traveling on the Great Wagon Road

The Great Wagon Road extended from Pennsylvania to South Carolina. Travel along the hilly route was difficult, and journeys lasted at least two months. Even the fastest wagon traveled only five miles a day. Often people crossed rivers by wading through them while guiding their wagons or carrying supplies. Although the weather was harsh, people frequently made the trip in winter because it was easier to travel on the frozen roads. Each year the Great Wagon Road stretched farther south, so that by 1775 it was close to 600 miles long. In the decade before the American Revolution, tens of thousands of settlers journeyed down the road in search of new opportunities. During this time, the Great Wagon Road was the most heavily traveled road in the colonies.

1 __F__ Settlements along the Great Wagon Road included York, Harrisonburg, Salisbury, and New York City.

2 __T__ Salisbury is located on the east side of the Great Wagon Road in North Carolina.

3 __T__ People frequently journeyed along the Great Wagon Road in the winter because it was easier to travel on the frozen roads.

4 __T__ The Great Wagon Road ran through parts of five different colonies.

5 __F__ The fastest wagons journeying on the Great Wagon Road traveled 25 miles a day.

6 Compare and contrast travel on American highways today with travel along the Great Wagon Road in the mid-1700s. Answers will vary. Students may mention their personal travel experiences and travel conditions compared to those of the Great Wagon Road.

_____

_____

_____

© Harcourt

Chapter Review

Directions Complete this graphic organizer by using information you have learned from the chapter to make inferences about the **Middle Atlantic Colonies** and the **backcountry.**

Breadbasket Colonies

WHAT YOU HAVE READ | **WHAT YOU KNOW**

The Middle Atlantic Colonies attracted people from many different backgrounds.

Many people in your classroom or school are from different backgrounds.

The Middle Atlantic Colonies had a blend of many heritages.

_____

_____

Moving West

WHAT YOU HAVE READ | **WHAT YOU KNOW**

Colonists who settled land farther west faced many challenges.

Sometimes it can be difficult adjusting to new places and surroundings.

People who settled the West overcame these challenges and successfully adjusted.

_____

_____

© Harcourt

Name _____ Date _____

6 Test Preparation

Directions Read each question and choose the best answer. Then fill in the circle for the answer you have chosen. Be sure to fill in the circle completely.

1 Farmers depended on _____ as places to trade their surplus farm produce.
- Ⓐ crops
- Ⓑ agriculture
- Ⓒ market towns
- Ⓓ meetinghouses

2 Philadelphia's location near good land and _____ was one reason it became Pennsylvania's main port.
- Ⓕ waterways
- Ⓖ wagon roads
- Ⓗ oceans
- Ⓙ fertile soil

3 The English and the _____ who came with William Penn were the largest groups of immigrants in Philadelphia.
- Ⓐ Puritans
- Ⓑ Catholics
- Ⓒ Quakers
- Ⓓ Shakers

4 The land between the Coastal Plain and the Appalachian Mountains is called the—
- Ⓕ farmland.
- Ⓖ backcountry.
- Ⓗ city.
- Ⓙ Fall Line.

5 Backcountry family members all had to do jobs or chores, such as—
- Ⓐ chopping wood.
- Ⓑ hunting.
- Ⓒ candle making.
- Ⓓ all of the above.

Use after reading Chapter 6, pages 210–227.

Settlement of the South

Directions Use the Word Bank to provide the missing information in the chart.

to make money from cash crops	Catholic landowners
the Lords Proprietors	James Oglethorpe
to give debtors a new start	French Huguenots
divided into two colonies	freedom to worship
1633	English

Settling the Southern Colonies

Where	Who	Why	When
Maryland	Founders: the Calverts, Catholic landowners First proprietor: Cecilius Calvert First governor: Leonard Calvert	freedom to worship	1633
Carolina	First proprietors: the Lords Proprietors (8 English nobles) First colonists: English settlers, settlers from the Caribbean, and French Huguenots First governor: William Drummond	to make money from cash crops	1663 1712: divided into two colonies
Georgia	First proprietors: James Oglethorpe and 19 partners First colonists: English	to give debtors a new start	1733

(continued)

Use after reading Chapter 7, Lesson 1, pages 232–239.

© Harcourt

Name _____ Date _____

Directions Use the chart on the preceding page to help you write answers to the questions.

1 Which colony wanted to help debtors? Georgia

2 What happened in Carolina in 1712? It divided into two colonies, North and

South Carolina.

3 Who were the Calverts? What colony did they found?

Catholic landowners; Maryland Colony

4 What freedom did the colonists of Maryland want? freedom to worship

5 Who were the Lords Proprietors, and what was their role in the colony?

8 English nobles who governed the Carolina Colony.

6 From what country were the Huguenots? France

7 What colony grew cash crops? Why do you think cash crops were important to

the colonists? Carolina; Possible answer: They provided the colonies with money

and allowed them to prosper.

Name _____ Date _____

READING SKILLS
Tell Fact From Opinion

Directions Read the paragraph below. Use the information in the paragraph to identify each statement as Fact or Opinion. In the blanks, write *F* if the statement is a fact and write *O* if the statement is an opinion.

James Oglethorpe

While a lawmaker in England, James Oglethorpe heard that a good friend had been sent to prison for not paying his debts. Oglethorpe hurried to the prison but arrived too late. His friend had died of smallpox. In memory of this friend, Oglethorpe decided to help debtors. One way he did this was by bringing debtors to the new colony of Georgia. Oglethorpe offered each settler a 50-acre bonus for every debtor that the settler brought along to help with the work of starting a colony. There the debtors could work for the settlers and pay back the money they owed. Oglethorpe hoped that debtors would work hard if they were given a second chance.

1 __F__ James Oglethorpe was a lawmaker in England.

2 __F__ A good friend of Oglethorpe's was in prison.

3 __F__ Oglethorpe did not arrive in time to help his friend.

4 __O__ Smallpox is the worst of all diseases.

5 __F__ Oglethorpe decided to help debtors.

6 __O__ Oglethorpe's idea to help debtors was a good one.

7 __O__ Hard work would benefit the debtors.

8 __F__ Debtors came to the Georgia Colony.

9 __O__ Oglethorpe was a good man.

Use after reading Chapter 7, Skill Lesson, page 240.

Southern Plantations

Directions Read the sentences below and decide whether the information applies to slaves or indentured servants. Circle the letter under the appropriate column. Then write that letter in the appropriate blank below.

Plantation Workers	Slaves	Indentured Servants
1 Sent by the English courts to work in the colonies to pay for their crimes	S	(W)
2 Kidnapped and sold in the colonies	(E)	M
3 Came willingly to the English colonies	O	(D)
4 Sold like property at auctions	(R)	U
5 Were given their freedom after a certain length of time	H	(A)
6 Were punished by overseers if they did not work hard	(T)	C
7 Had little money to travel, so they went with others and worked off their debts	N	(T)
8 Two kinds of these workers existed: field and house	(E)	P
9 Were forbidden by law to learn how to read and write	(I)	J

Where were the earliest plantations usually built?

```
 T    I    D    E    W    A    T    E    R
___  ___  ___  ___  ___  ___  ___  ___  ___
 6    9    3    8    1    5    7    2    4
```

Name _____   Date _____

MAP AND GLOBE SKILLS
Read a Resource and Product Map

Products of the East Coast

Lake Superior

Lake Michigan

Lake Huron

Lake Ontario

Lake Erie

N
W — E
S

ME

VT   NH

NY   Portland
      Portsmouth
      Boston

MA
RI
      Newport

CT

PA   New York City

Philadelphia   NJ

Baltimore   DE

DC MD

VA

Norfolk

NC

Charlotte

SC

GA   Charleston

Savannah

ATLANTIC OCEAN

🍎	Apples
🫐	Blueberries
🐂	Cattle
🌽	Corn
🐄	Dairy
⬭	Eggs
🐖	Hogs
🌲	Nursery products
🥜	Peanuts
🐓	Poultry
🦐	Seafood
🫘	Soybeans
🌿	Tobacco
🥬	Vegetables

(continued)

Use after reading Chapter 7, Skill Lesson, pages 246–247.

Name _____ Date _____

Directions **Use the map on page 68 to help you answer the questions.**

1 What product is produced in every state? dairy _____

2 Where on the East Coast will you find tobacco grown? Virginia, North Carolina,
South Carolina

3 In which state are blueberries grown? Maine _____

4 Where on the East Coast will you find apples grown? Maine, New Hampshire,
Vermont, New York

5 Where are soybeans grown? Delaware, North Carolina, South Carolina,
Maryland, Virginia

6 Which two states grow exactly the same kinds of products?
Virginia and South Carolina

7 In which state are peanuts grown? Georgia _____

8 What products are produced in South Carolina that are not produced in Maine?
tobacco, hogs, and soybeans

Use the map to explain what opportunities there might be for a person looking for a
job in the southern states.

Answers should show that there are many kinds of industries to choose from in

that area: tobacco, dairy, hogs, peanuts, poultry and eggs, nursery stock, and

soybeans. Students may be aware that hog farming is a huge business in North

Carolina and that nursery stock is always in demand. The dairy industry has been

growing rapidly in recent years. Dairy and hog farming and raising poultry for their

meat or eggs all are big businesses.

Use after reading Chapter 7, Skill Lesson, pages 246–247.

Name _____ Date _____

Southern Cities

Directions Fill in each blank with the correct word.

1 Some workers specialized as fishers, tailors, printers, or ___hat makers___ .

2 A young person often learned a trade by becoming an ___apprentice___ .

3 ___Merchants___ and ___planters___ had the most power in Charles Town society.

4 What was one reason wealthy planters lived in Charles Town during the summer months? to get away from the summer insect infestations on their plantations' wetlands

5 What did colonists find when they moved north along the Atlantic coast in search of fertile soil for plantations? What did they do with their find?

They found a lot of trees. They eventually cut down trees and built sawmills.

6 Some of Wilmington's earliest immigrants came from ___northern Scotland___

_____ .

7 The Georgia Colony's chief port was the coastal town of ___Savannah___ .

8 What were the three products that caused Norfolk, Virginia, to grow quickly?

tobacco, naval stores, and lumber

9 In Baltimore the ___Patapsco___ River flows into the

___Chesapeake___ Bay.

10 What was the reason for Baltimore's successful shipyards?

improved ship building methods

Use after reading Chapter 7, Lesson 3, pages 248–251.

© Harcourt

The Southern Colonies

Directions Complete this graphic organizer by using facts you have learned from the chapter to make generalizations about the Southern Colonies.

1. Settlement of the South

FACTS				GENERALIZATION
By 1700 Virginia is the largest English colony in North America.	Transportation improves throughout Virginia.	Williamsburg becomes a large, well-planned city.	Williamsburg is now the cultural center of Virginia.	The Virginia Colony is the largest and busiest of the Southern Colonies.

2. Southern Plantations

FACTS				GENERALIZATION
Planters grow cash crops.	To grow more crops, planters start more plantations.	Planters trade cash crops for goods and services.	Planters sell their crops to England.	Plantations were important to the economy of the Southern Colonies.

3. Southern Cities

FACTS				GENERALIZATION
In 20 years Charles Town's population grows from 300 to 6,000 people.	Charles Town is the largest city in the Southern Colonies.	Most of the people in South Carolina live in or around Charles Town.	Merchants and planters are powerful members of Charles Town's society.	Charles Town was the busiest city in the Southern Colonies.

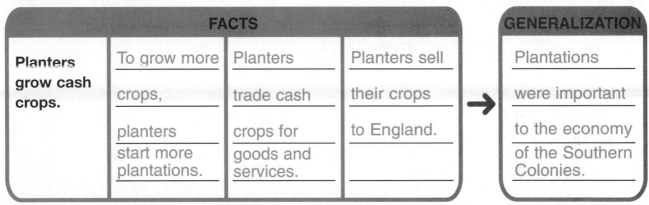

© Harcourt

Use after reading Chapter 7, pages 231–251.

Name _____ Date _____

7 Test Preparation

Directions Read each question and choose the best answer. Then fill in the circle for the answer you have chosen. Be sure to fill in the circle completely.

1 The Calverts wanted to build a colony in North America to make money and provide a refuge for _____.
- Ⓐ Puritans
- ⬤ Catholics
- Ⓒ colonists
- Ⓓ debtors

2 In the Carolina Colony, the Lords Proprietors wrote a _____, which was a written plan of government.
- Ⓕ charter
- Ⓖ action plan
- Ⓗ ratification
- ⬤ constitution

3 By the mid-1700s _____, Virginia, was one of the most important cities in the 13 colonies.
- ⬤ Williamsburg
- Ⓑ Savannah
- Ⓒ Baltimore
- Ⓓ Charles Town

4 _____ owners became important leaders in the 13 colonies.
- Ⓕ Ship
- Ⓖ Sawmill
- ⬤ Plantation
- Ⓙ Land

5 Unlike _____, indentured servants were not taken against their will and were given their freedom after a certain length of time.
- Ⓐ overseers
- ⬤ slaves
- Ⓒ debtors
- Ⓓ masters

© Harcourt

Use after reading Chapter 7, pages 230–253.

Name _____ Date _____

Ways of Life in Colonial Mexico and New France

Directions The colonies of New Spain and New France each had several social classes. Read the quotes below and write the name of the speaker's social class on the line. Use the charts and your textbook to help you identify each social class.

New France Social Classes

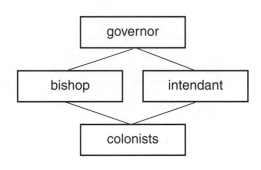

New Spain Social Classes

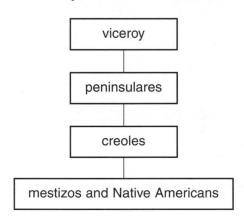

1 "My mother is a Native American and my father is a creole. In New Spain, I am part of a large lower social class." _mestizo_____

2 "I was born in Mexico and grew up to become Acapulco's best merchant and weaver. I learned the trades from my parents, who moved here from Spain 50 years ago." _creole_____

3 "I am not the governor of New France, but I manage the colonial government. I am responsible for the colony's law and order, financial matters, and public transportation." _intendant_____

4 "I lead the colony of New Spain. I was appointed by the king of Spain to be the colonial governor." _viceroy_____

5 "When we were younger, my wife and I moved to Mexico from Spain. Today my family is among Mexico's largest landowners." _peninsulares_____

© Harcourt

Name _____ Date _____

Directions The colonists of New France and New Spain built homes to fit their environments. Look at the terms related to these homes. Then write a sentence that describes how each helped the colonists survive.

1 adobe brick walls The clay-brick walls kept the house cool in the summer and warm in the winter.

2 wooden roof with drains The wooden roof with drains collected and carried off rainwater.

3 porch The porch offered shade and protection from rain and snow.

4 clay fireplace The fireplace was used for cooking and as a source of heat.

5 timber framework Large wooden beams supported the walls of the house.

6 brick walls Heavy brick walls offered protection and warmth.

7 large fireplaces The fireplaces were large enough to heat the entire house.

8 wooden shutters Wooden shutters helped keep out cold winds.

9 steep slopes on roofs Steep slopes on roofs let snow slide off.

10 stone required on houses Stone helped prevent the spread of fire from house to house.

© Harcourt

The French and Indian War Begins

Directions Read the passage below and complete the activities that follow.

General Braddock's Defeat

General Edward Braddock was appointed the commander of all British forces in the French and Indian War. His first goal was to capture Fort Duquesne, the French stronghold. In April 1755 he led more than 1,800 British and colonial troops westward across the mountains. The trip was long and difficult for the soldiers as they moved the large wagons and artillery across the rough trails.

Meanwhile, the French had learned of the British advance and were waiting. About 8 miles from Fort Duquesne, the French and their Native American allies attacked the British from behind trees and boulders. The British were trained to fight in open fields and had never fought an enemy this way. After the battle, almost two-thirds of the British troops were dead or wounded, including General Braddock. He died four days later.

Directions For numbers 1–5, write *T* next to the statements that are true and *F* next to the statements that are false.

1 __F__ General Braddock was the commander of all British forces in the Revolutionary War.

2 __T__ Braddock's army had a difficult journey to Fort Duquesne.

3 __T__ The French were aware that Braddock's army was approaching.

4 __F__ The British were trained to fight in wooded areas.

5 __F__ General Braddock died immediately after being wounded on the battlefield.

Directions For numbers 6–10, write *F* if the statement is a fact or *O* if the statement is an opinion.

6 __O__ The French were excellent fighters.

7 __F__ The Native Americans were allies of the French.

8 __O__ General Braddock was nervous about the journey to Fort Duquesne.

9 __F__ Moving large artillery was difficult.

10 __F__ Braddock's army consisted of British and colonial troops.

Britain Wins North America

Directions Number the sentences below in the order in which each event occurred.

__5__ To make up for Spain's losses in the war, France gave Spain most of Louisiana and part of what is now Florida.

__7__ Native Americans did not welcome the British colonists who wanted to settle in the Ohio Valley after the Treaty of Paris was signed.

__1__ The British captured three forts: Fort Duquesne, Louisbourg, and Frontenac.

__6__ The French and Indian War ended with the Treaty of Paris, giving Britain control of lands in present-day Canada and the area between the Appalachian Mountains and the Mississippi River.

__9__ Many Native American fighters signed peace treaties with the British.

__3__ French forces were defeated by General James Wolfe's British troops on the Plains of Abraham, near Quebec.

__4__ The French gave up after the British captured Montreal.

__2__ The British captured forts at Crown Point, Niagara, and Ticonderoga.

__8__ Chief Pontiac united with other Native American tribes and attacked British forts.

__10__ King George III issued the Proclamation of 1763, which prevented British colonists from buying, hunting on, or exploring land west of the Appalachian Mountains.

(continued)

Directions   **Write your answer to each question.**

1 Why did King George III order the Proclamation of 1763?

King George believed that stopping the westward movement of British colonists

was the only way to prevent more wars between the colonists and Native

Americans.

2 What effects did the proclamation have on the life of the British colonists?

The land west of the Appalachians was off-limits to the colonists. They could no

longer buy, hunt on, or explore it; any colonist already living there was ordered

to leave.

3 How did the American colonists feel about the proclamation? Why did they feel

this way?   It angered the colonists because they felt the proclamation took away

their right as British citizens to travel where they wanted.

_____

4 According to the British colonists, how did the Proclamation of 1763 conflict with

the English Bill of Rights?   The English Bill of Rights gave the colonists the same

rights as all British citizens. The colonists believed the proclamation took away

these rights.

5 Did the proclamation stop colonists from settling west of the Appalachians?

Explain.   No. Even though colonists were not supposed to use the land, colonial

pioneers continued to push westward into the frontier.

_____

Use after reading Chapter 8, Lesson 2, pages 273–277.

MAP AND GLOBE SKILLS

Compare Historical Maps

Directions Use the maps to answer the questions on both pages.

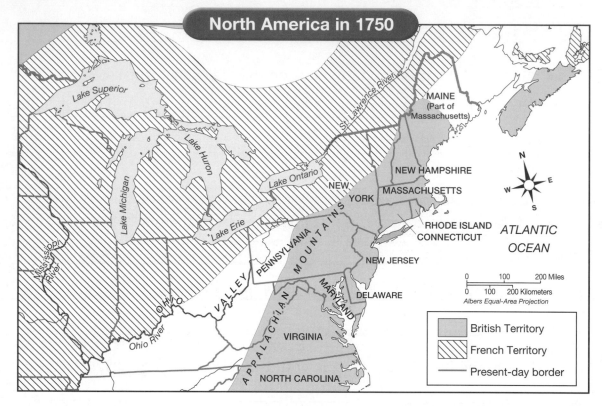

North America in 1750

1. What pattern is used to show land originally claimed by the British and then given to the Native Americans? hatch lines

2. According to the map, was any land claimed by the French in North America in 1763? no

3. What land areas once claimed by the French were later claimed by the British?
the land near the Mississippi River

4. Before the French and Indian War, who occupied the territory along the St. Lawrence River? the French

5. Before 1763, who claimed most of the land north of the Ohio River?
the French

(continued)

Use after reading Chapter 8, Skill Lesson, pages 278–279.

© Harcourt

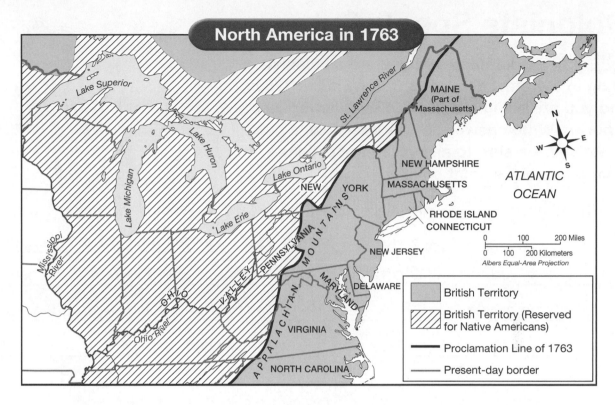

North America in 1763

6 Who claimed the region of present-day Kentucky after the French and

Indian War? _the British_____

7 When did the British claim the regions bordering the Atlantic Ocean, such as

Massachusetts, Connecticut, and Rhode Island? _both before and after the____

French and Indian War_____

8 Imagine that you are an explorer living in 1750. Write a description of the
following journey: You start in what is now Maine and travel to the New York
Colony, then to the region now known as Michigan, and then to the Ohio Valley
region. How did you travel? Who claimed the land in which you traveled?
What direction did you take? What kind of people did you encounter?

Student answers will vary. Possible answer: I would travel by land or by boat

to New York. Then journey across New York to the Great Lakes and into Michigan

and the Ohio Valley. My journey began in British territory then moved into French

territory. I encountered other colonists, Native Americans, and some French and

British troops.

© Harcourt

Colonists Speak Out

Directions Imagine that you are a colonist living in the Massachusetts Colony in the 1760s and you are being interviewed by a newspaper reporter. Write answers to the interview questions. Be sure to answer the questions from a colonist's point of view.

1 Many people like you are angry about the Sugar Act. What is the Sugar Act, and why has it angered you? Possible answer: The Sugar Act adds taxes on sugar and other goods coming to the colonies from other places. This means we have to pay more for goods. The act angers me and my fellow colonists because we believe our rights as British citizens have been violated.

2 Soon after the Sugar Act, the Stamp Act was enacted. How is the Stamp Act similar to the Sugar Act? Possible answer: Both acts force us to pay taxes. Again, we feel our rights as British citizens have been violated.

3 What can you do to show you are against taxation without representation? Possible answer: Many of us are refusing to buy goods that have been stamped. We are also boycotting many British goods. Some women in our town are making their own cloth so that we do not have to buy cloth from Britain.

4 Why are there so many British soldiers in Massachusetts and the other colonies? How do you feel about the soldiers being here? Possible answer: Parliament is trying to show its authority over us by sending many soldiers. Having these soldiers here angers not only me but also my fellow colonists.

© Harcourt

Name _____   Date _____

CITIZENSHIP SKILLS
Determine Point of View

Directions Read each statement and then decide whose point of view the statement represents. Write either "Colonist" or "British leader" in the blank space before the sentence. In the second blank space, explain why each person might hold this point of view.

1 _____British leader_____ We need money to help pay the cost of the French and Indian War.

The British Parliament discussed this in its 1764 budget before it passed new laws that taxed the colonists.

2 _____Colonist_____ The Sugar Act is unjust. We had no representation when this law was decided.

The colonists did not have a voice in Parliament and believed their rights had been violated.

3 _____British leader_____ Patrick Henry has committed treason. He is working against his government.

British leaders in the colonies thought Patrick Henry was against the government because he did not agree with Parliament's new laws.

4 _____Colonist_____ We need to work together instead of acting separately. We should talk with other colonial leaders to discuss what to do about the Stamp Act.

Colonial leaders thought it was better for the colonies to work together, so they held a meeting. Nine colonies sent representatives to this meeting to talk about the new taxes.

5 _____Colonist_____ We do not want "lobsters" and "redcoats" in our cities!

Colonists were angry at the great numbers of British soldiers being sent to the 13 colonies.

© Harcourt

Use after reading Chapter 8, Skill Lesson, pages 286–287.

Name _____ Date _____

The Road to War

Directions Use the Word Bank to complete each sentence.

Lexington	quarter
Samuel Adams	monopoly
Minutemen	Sons of Liberty
petition	Paul Revere
Intolerable Acts	blockade

1 Parliament wanted to give the East India Company a _____ monopoly _____ on tea.

2 _____ Samuel Adams _____ believed in the use of violence only when all else failed.

3 A group of men called the _____ Sons of Liberty _____ boarded ships and dumped tea into the harbor.

4 To keep ships from entering or leaving Boston Harbor, Parliament ordered a _____ blockade _____.

5 Colonists were punished by having to _____ quarter _____ British soldiers.

6 The colonists called Parliament's new laws the _____ Intolerable Acts _____.

7 The First Continental Congress sent Parliament a _____ petition _____, which stated that colonists had a right to "life, liberty, and property."

8 Colonists in Massachusetts organized a militia made up of _____ Minutemen _____.

9 When he learned the British were coming, _____ Paul Revere _____ rode to Lexington to warn fellow colonists.

10 The fighting at _____ Lexington _____ and Concord marked the beginning of the Revolutionary War.

© Harcourt

Use after reading Chapter 8, Lesson 4, pages 288–292.

The Second Continental Congress

Directions Imagine that you are a member of the Second Continental Congress. Write a letter to King George III explaining why you believe the colonies in North America should be allowed to peacefully separate from Britain.

Think about these questions as you write your letter:

What was John Dickinson's point of view on war?

How many people died in the battle at Breed's Hill?

How might a petition help?

Who, other than the British and colonists, might be affected by war?

Students' letters may indicate that a peaceful separation is better because it avoids many deaths. They may also argue that too many people have died already. They may explain that a petition is a peaceful approach to solving a problem. They may indicate that Native Americans will be caught up in the war.

Events Unite the Colonies

Directions Complete this graphic organizer to show that you understand the causes and effects of some of the key events that helped unite the colonies.

Cause		Effect

The British Parliament needs extra money to pay for the French and Indian War.	The British Parliament taxes the colonists.

Colonists are angry about the British government's tax on tea.	The Boston Tea Party takes place in Boston Harbor in December 1773.

The British Parliament passes the Intolerable Acts to punish the colonists.	The First Continental Congress is held.

The Minutemen and the British fight at Lexington and Concord.	The Second Continental Congress is held in Philadelphia in May 1775.

The Battle of Bunker Hill takes place near Boston on June 17, 1775.	Britain's King George III issues a proclamation of rebellion.

© Harcourt

Use after reading Chapter 8, pages 267–297.

Name _____   Date _____

8 Test Preparation

Directions Read each question and choose the best answer. Then fill in the circle for the answer you have chosen. Be sure to fill in the circle completely.

1 The French and Indian War began because both France and Britain believed they owned the area known as—
- Ⓐ Pennsylvania.
- Ⓑ the Appalachians.
- Ⓒ the Ohio Valley.
- Ⓓ New France.

2 Chief Pontiac's rebellion began because he—
- Ⓕ believed he owned the Ohio Valley region.
- Ⓖ wanted to stop the loss of Indian hunting lands.
- Ⓗ had formed an alliance with France.
- Ⓙ wanted to rule British forts.

3 Why were colonists angered by the tax laws passed by the British Parliament?
- Ⓐ They believed they should have a voice in deciding such laws.
- Ⓑ They were too poor to pay the taxes.
- Ⓒ They thought the taxes were unfair.
- Ⓓ They believed they shouldn't have to pay any taxes.

4 Which of the following was an Intolerable Act?
- Ⓕ preventing the Massachusetts legislature from making laws
- Ⓖ banning any town meetings not authorized by the governor
- Ⓗ forcing colonists to quarter British soldiers
- Ⓙ all of the above

5 The first united colonial army was called—
- Ⓐ the Continental Army.
- Ⓑ the Hessian Army.
- Ⓒ the Mercenary Army.
- Ⓓ the Loyalist Army.

© Harcourt

Use after reading Chapter 8, pages 268–297.

Independence Is Declared

Directions Use words and phrases from the Word Bank to complete each sentence below.

| public opinion | Preamble | resolution |
| allegiance | independence | grievances |

1 The point of view held by most people is called _____public opinion_____.

2 The colonists wanted _____independence_____, the freedom to govern themselves.

3 Another word for loyalty is _____allegiance_____.

4 Richard Henry Lee wrote a formal statement, known as a _____resolution_____, describing the feelings of the colonists.

5 The first part of the Declaration of Independence is called the _____Preamble_____.

6 The complaints, or _____grievances_____, against the British king and Parliament were part of the Declaration of Independence.

(continued)

Name _____ Date _____

Directions Match each person with the correct description. Write the letter of the correct person on the blank provided. Some letters may be used more than once.

Description		Name
7 ___D___ first to sign the Declaration of Independence		**A.** John Dickinson
8 ___F___ wrote the Declaration of Independence		**B.** John Adams
9 ___B___ wrote a letter to his wife Abigail describing the first public reading of the Declaration of Independence		**C.** John Nixon
10 ___E___ published *Common Sense* in January, 1776		**D.** John Hancock
11 ___A___ helped write the Articles of the Confederation		**E.** Thomas Paine
12 ___C___ read the Declaration of Independence to the Second Continental Congress		**F.** Thomas Jefferson
13 ___F___ wrote *A Summary View of the Rights of British America*		
14 ___E___ called for a revolution before the Declaration of Independence was written		

Americans and the Revolution

Directions Read the passage below. When you have finished, write a paragraph trying to persuade someone to choose a different position in the Revolutionary War. For example, you may try to persuade a Loyalist to become a Patriot.

As the Revolutionary War began, most colonists held one of four opinions. Those who supported the British king and Parliament were called **Loyalists.** They wanted to work out the differences between the colonies and Britain. Those people who were **Patriots** wanted to break from Britain and form a new country. They believed they could establish a better government if they were independent.

Some people wanted to wait and see what would happen. They did not want to take either side. They were **neutral** about the matter of independence and willing to accept whatever happened. Some people, such as Quakers, were opposed to war for any reason. They were known as **pacifists,** or people who believe in settling disagreements peacefully.

© Harcourt

CITIZENSHIP SKILLS
Make a Decision

Directions The Revolutionary War has begun. How will you respond? Explain your decision, based on the questions below.

Steps in Making a Decision

1 Know that you have to make a decision.

You have the choice of fighting for the British or for the colonists.

2 Gather information.

What do you need to know before deciding? Where might you find the information you need?

Students should state that they need to know what each side is fighting for.

Students should state that they could find this information by talking to people.

3 Identify your choices.

There are at least two choices, as given above. Are there other choices you could make?

Students' answers should include remaining neutral or taking a pacifist position.

4 Predict consequences, and weigh those consequences.

List each of the choices with its consequences. If a consequence seems very important to you, put a star next to it.

Students' answers will vary, but should indicate which consequence seems most

important to them.

5 Make a choice, and take action.

What will you decide?

Students' answers will vary but should give reasons that support their decisions.

© Harcourt

Fighting the Revolutionary War

Directions Follow the instructions below. Write your answers on the map.

1 Draw a star next to the battle known as the turning point of the war. Saratoga

2 Circle the place where Ethan Allen and the Green Mountain boys were victorious. Fort Ticonderoga

3 Draw a snowflake next to the place where Washington's troops spent the winter of 1777. Valley Forge

4 Draw a pitcher at the battle where Mary Ludwig Hays McCauley brought water to the soldiers. Monmouth

5 Draw a boat where Washington surprised Hessian mercenaries on Christmas Day, 1776. Trenton

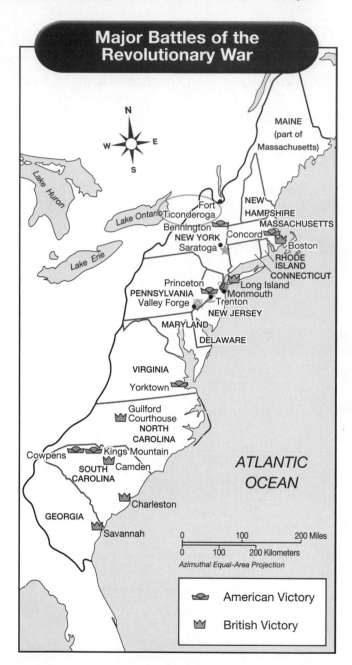

Major Battles of the Revolutionary War

MAINE (part of Massachusetts)

Lake Huron

Lake Ontario

Fort Ticonderoga

NEW HAMPSHIRE

Bennington

NEW YORK

Concord

MASSACHUSETTS

Saratoga

Boston

RHODE ISLAND

Lake Erie

CONNECTICUT

Princeton

Long Island

PENNSYLVANIA

Monmouth

Valley Forge

Trenton

NEW JERSEY

MARYLAND

DELAWARE

VIRGINIA

Yorktown

Guilford Courthouse

NORTH CAROLINA

Cowpens

Kings Mountain

SOUTH CAROLINA

Camden

Charleston

GEORGIA

Savannah

ATLANTIC OCEAN

0   100   200 Miles
0   100   200 Kilometers
Azimuthal Equal-Area Projection

American Victory

British Victory

Use after reading Chapter 9, Lesson 3, pages 314–319.

© Harcourt

Independence Is Won

Directions Complete the time line using the choices listed below. Write the number of the event next to the correct marker on the time line.

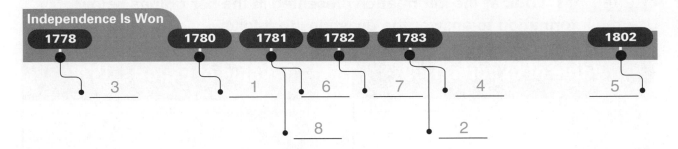

Independence Is Won

| 1778 | 1780 | 1781 | 1782 | 1783 | 1802 |

3 _____   1 _____   6 _____   7 _____   4 _____   5 _____

8 _____   2 _____

1 British capture Charleston, South Carolina 1780

2 George Washington returns to Virginia 1783

3 British capture Savannah, Georgia 1778

4 Britain and the United States sign the Treaty of Paris 1783

5 The United States Military Academy is founded at West Point 1802

6 British surrender at Yorktown 1781

7 Britain and the United States send representatives to Paris 1782

8 The Continental Army wins the Battle of Cowpens 1781

© Harcourt

Name _____ Date _____

CHART AND GRAPH SKILLS
Compare Graphs

Directions Look at the information presented in the bar graphs below. Use the information to answer the questions that follow.

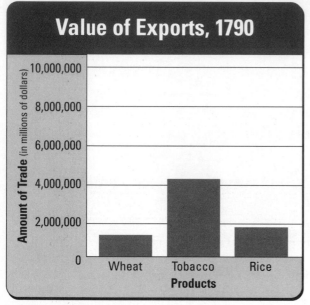

Value of Exports, 1790

Amount of Trade (in millions of dollars)

| 10,000,000 |
| 8,000,000 |
| 6,000,000 |
| 4,000,000 |
| 2,000,000 |
| 0 | Wheat | Tobacco | Rice |

Products

Source: *A History of Commerce* by Clive Day Longmans, Green and Co.

Value of Exports, 1998

Amount of Trade (in billions of dollars)

| 10,000,000 |
| 8,000,000 |
| 6,000,000 |
| 4,000,000 |
| 2,000,000 |
| 0 | Wheat | Tobacco | Rice |

Products

Source: Statistical Abstract of the United States

1 Compare the two graphs. How has the relative importance of each item's dollar value changed? <u>Answers may vary. Students may point out that wheat was once the smallest export but now is the most important in value. Others may point out that tobacco is no longer the country's leading agricultural export.</u>

2 About how much more valuable were tobacco exports compared to wheat exports in 1790? <u>about 2.7 million dollars</u>

3 About how much more valuable were wheat exports compared to tobacco exports in 1998? <u>about 2.4 billion dollars</u>

(continued)

Use after reading Chapter 9, Skill Lesson, pages 330–331.

© Harcourt

Name _____ Date _____

Directions Look at the information presented in the line graphs below.
Use the graphs to answer the questions that follow.

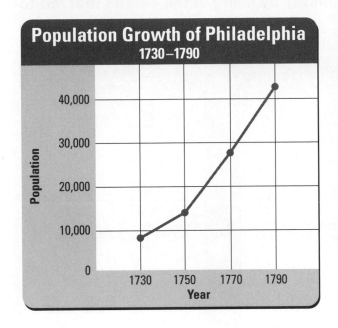

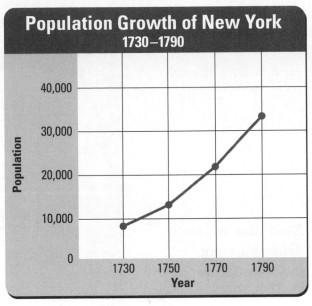

4 Which city grew faster from 1730 to 1790? Philadelphia _____

5 In what years were the two cities equal or nearly equal in population?

1730 and 1750 _____

6 In 1770, about how many more people lived in Philadelphia than in New York?

about 7,000 _____

7 By how many times did the population of Philadelphia grow over the 60 years

the graph covers? The population grew about five times its original size. _____

8 What was the growth in New York during the same time period?

The population grew to about four times its original size. _____

© Harcourt

Independence Is Declared

Directions Complete this graphic organizer by filling in the events that led to the colonies declaring independence.

FIRST	NEXT	LAST
Colonists in North America want independence for the 13 British Colonies →	Congress approves and signs the Declaration of Independence	The 13 American Colonies declare their independence from the British

Use after reading Chapter 9, pages 301–331.

9 Test Preparation

Directions Read each question and choose the best answer. Then fill in the circle for the answer you have chosen. Be sure to fill in the circle completely.

1 Which of the following was **not** a reason American colonists wanted to break with Britain in 1776?
- Ⓐ taxes
- Ⓑ no representation
- Ⓒ religious freedom
- Ⓓ war had already begun

2 Who was the author of the Declaration of Independence?
- Ⓕ Thomas Paine
- Ⓖ John Adams
- Ⓗ Richard Henry Lee
- Ⓙ Thomas Jefferson

3 People who remained neutral in the war—
- Ⓐ sided with the colonists.
- Ⓑ took neither side.
- Ⓒ did not believe war was right.
- Ⓓ were loyal to Britain.

4 Which of the following countries did **not** send help to the colonies?
- Ⓕ Scotland
- Ⓖ France
- Ⓗ Poland
- Ⓙ Spain

5 General Cornwallis surrendered at the Battle of—
- Ⓐ Fort Ticonderoga.
- Ⓑ Saratoga.
- Ⓒ Charlestown.
- Ⓓ Yorktown.

© Harcourt

Use after reading Chapter 9, pages 300–331.

From Colonies to Nations

Directions The statements listed below describe specific events related to independence for the countries of Central America and the Caribbean. Place the events in correct time order by numbering them from 1 to 10.

1 ___8___ The United Provinces of Central America become independent countries.

2 ___1___ The American and French Revolutions show Mexicans that freedom from Spain is possible.

3 ___10___ Britain grants independence to Belize in 1981.

4 ___3___ A Mexican congress declares independence from Spain.

5 ___6___ The Central American countries form the United Provinces of Central America.

6 ___9___ Fidel Castro overthrows Cuba's dictator.

7 ___4___ Members of Spain's royal family refuse to lead the newly independent Mexico.

8 ___7___ Guadelupe Victoria is elected Mexico's first president.

9 ___2___ Father Hidalgo calls for Mexican independence.

10 ___5___ Augustín de Iturbide is declared Emperor of Mexico.

Use after reading Unit 4, pages U4-1 to U4-15.

© Harcourt

Name _____ Date _____

Directions Canada achieved full independence from British rule in 1982.
Below are causes and effects of ten events in Canadian history. Match each
cause with an effect by writing the letter of the effect on the line provided.

CAUSES

1. __C__ Britain and France began fighting the French and Indian War in 1754.

2. __G__ In Canada, Britain wanted to avoid the kinds of problems it faced with
the 13 colonies.

3. __A__ Britain passed the Quebec Act, giving many rights to the French Canadians.

4. __B__ Many Loyalists moved to Nova Scotia after the American Revolution.

5. __D__ Loyalists in Quebec wanted their own colony.

6. __F__ Canadians worried that the United States might expand into Canada.

7. __H__ In 1869 Canada purchased Rupert's Land from the Hudson's Bay Company.

8. __E__ Canadians felt a sense of pride as the country increased in size.

9. __J__ In 1965 the Canadian government chose a new national flag.

10. __I__ The British government approved the Constitution Act.

EFFECTS

A. People in the 13 British colonies became angry.

B. The Loyalists were given their own colony,
called New Brunswick.

C. The British won control of New France in 1763.

D. The British divided Quebec into Upper Canada and Lower Canada.

E. Canadians began to think of themselves as Canadian rather than British.

F. The British North America Act of 1867 created the Dominion of Canada.

G. Britain passed the Quebec Act.

H. The provinces of Manitoba, Alberta, and Saskatchewan were formed.

I. Canada gained full independence from Britain.

J. Canada's new flag showed its own Canadian identity.

© Harcourt

The Confederation Period

Directions Each statement below is false. For each sentence, cross out the wrong word. Then, in the blank at the end of the sentence, write the word that would make the sentence true.

1 After the war with Britain ended, Congress printed too much money, causing terrible ~~rebellion~~. _inflation_

2 A form of government in which people elect representatives to govern the country is called a ~~dictatorship~~. _republic_

3 Decision making required representation from at least ~~five~~ states.
nine

4 Shays's Rebellion started over ~~army policy~~. _taxes_

5 Shays's Rebellion took place in ~~Virginia~~. _Massachusetts_

6 An arsenal is a place to store ~~food~~. _weapons_

7 A territory is land that belongs to the ~~state~~ government but is not represented in Congress. _national_

8 Congress passed an ~~arsenal~~, or set of laws, to measure the western lands.
ordinance

9 The newly settled lands were called the ~~Southeast~~ Territory.
Northwest

10 Townships were ~~8~~ miles on each side. _6_

11 The new lands were to offer ~~private~~ schools to everyone.
public

Use after reading Chapter 10, Lesson 1, pages 346–350.

© Harcourt

The Constitutional Convention

Directions Read the following list of issues debated at the Constitutional Convention. Match the resolution of each one with the correct issue. Write the letter of the correct resolution on the blank provided.

1 __B__ the relationship between the states and national government

2 __C__ representation of each state in Congress

3 __A__ the issue of enslaved African Americans

A. the Three-Fifths Compromise

B. a federal system of shared powers

C. a system of two houses of Congress

Directions Read each sentence below, and fill in the blank with the correct term. Use the words from the Word Bank.

George Read	George Washington	Roger Sherman
Rhode Island	Benjamin Franklin	

4 All the states except _____Rhode Island_____ sent delegates to Philadelphia.

5 The oldest member of the convention was _____Benjamin Franklin_____ .

6 The delegates elected _____George Washington_____ president of the convention.

7 _____George Read_____ believed that states should be done away with altogether.

8 The Connecticut Compromise was created by _____Roger Sherman_____ .

© Harcourt

The Three Branches of Government

Directions Read the list below of positions in the government. In the space provided, name the correct branch of government for each one. Then write a brief description of the qualifications and duties of the person holding that job.

1 President Executive; serves for 4 years, must be at least 35 years old, must have been born in the United States or have parents who were born in the United States. A President has veto power, is commander in chief of the armed forces, and represents the country to other nations.

2 Supreme Court Justice Judicial; appointed by the President for life, subject to Senate approval; hears cases dealing with the Constitution, national law, or treaties.

3 Representative Legislative; serves for 2 years, must be at least 25 years old, must have been a citizen for 7 years, must live in the state he or she represents. Representatives can make laws, declare war, coin money, and originate tax bills.

© Harcourt

Name _____ Date _____

CHART AND GRAPH SKILLS
Read a Flow Chart

Directions Fill in the flow chart to show the jobs in each of the three branches of government. In the second row, describe the main task of each branch. Some examples have been filled in for you.

EXECUTIVE	LEGISLATIVE		JUDICIAL
President _____ _____	Senator	Representative _____ _____	Supreme Court Justice _____
to enforce the laws	to make laws _____ _____		to interpret laws _____ _____

© Harcourt

Name _____   Date _____

Approval and the Bill of Rights

Directions Read the freedoms guaranteed by the Bill of Rights. Then read each statement that follows. If the statement is a fact, write *F* in the blank. If the statement is an opinion, write *O* in the blank.

1. People may follow any religion. The government cannot financially support or promote any religion. People have freedom to speak, to publish, and to hold meetings.

2. People may keep and bear weapons.

3. People do not have to board soldiers in their homes during peacetime.

4. The government cannot search people's homes or remove their property without the permission of a judge.

5–8. People have the right to a fair trial by a jury. Defendants do not have to testify against themselves. They may have a lawyer represent them in court. They cannot be tried twice for the same crime.

9. People have other rights not specifically listed in the Constitution.

10. The federal government can do only what the Constitution gives it permission to do. All other powers belong to the states and to the people.

1 ___O___ It is not fair to have soldiers sleeping in your home at any time.

2 ___F___ People can hold public meetings to talk about their government.

3 ___O___ Newspapers should print only good news.

4 ___O___ The federal government has gotten too powerful.

5 ___F___ A person cannot be tried twice for the same crime.

6 ___O___ The individual states do not have enough power.

7 ___F___ People do not have to testify against themselves in court.

Name _____   Date _____

CITIZENSHIP SKILLS
Act as a Responsible Citizen

Directions Citizens have responsibilities as well as rights and privileges. Read each statement below the picture. Then suggest how a responsible citizen might handle the situation.

1 You notice that people are being careless about litter in your neighborhood.

Answers will vary but may suggest picking up litter, organizing a group to

monitor litter, or petitioning for more trash containers to be placed in public areas.

2 Several dogs in your neighborhood are not on leashes.

Answers will vary but may suggest creating or enforcing leash laws.

3 Skateboarders in your neighborhood are practicing on sidewalks and in the street.

Answers will vary but may suggest trying to persuade local officials to designate

a skateboard park area.

4 A local election is coming up. Answers will vary but should indicate that a

responsible citizen would vote.

5 A new law is coming up for discussion before being voted on. Some people

disagree with the law. Answers will vary but may suggest writing a letter to the

editor of a local newspaper or attending local political meetings to express

opinions.

© Harcourt

The New Government Begins

Directions The two major political parties of the late eighteenth century differed in several ways. Fill out the chart below to show how they were different. One example has been given.

FEDERALIST	REPUBLICAN
Believed in a strong central government	Believed that the powers of the national government should be limited to those stated in the Constitution
Answers may include the following:	Answers may include the following:
Believed government should	Believed the economy should
encourage manufacturing; Believed	depend on agriculture; Believed the
the United States should have close	United States should have close
ties with Britain; Wanted a federal	ties with France; Wanted little
bank to issue paper money; Were	government; Were followers
followers of Hamilton	of Jefferson

Use after reading Chapter 10, Lesson 5, pages 374–379.

© Harcourt

A New Form of Government

Directions Complete this graphic organizer by summarizing the facts about the writing and ratification of the United States Constitution.

TOPIC OR EVENT

The Constitutional Convention

→

IMPORTANT DETAILS

What?

A convention to discuss the Articles of Confederation

Who?
Delegates from 12 of the 13 United States

Where?

Philadelphia

How?

in secret

Why?

to discuss the many

ideas delegates

attending the

convention had on

how to improve the

Articles of

Confederation

→

SUMMARY

Delegates to the

Philadelphia

Convention met to

discuss ways to

improve upon the

Articles of

Confederation.

Instead, the

Convention

delegates decided to

do away with the

Articles and create a

new form of

government.

_____

_____

Name _____ Date _____

10 Test Preparation

Directions Read each question and choose the best answer. Then fill in the circle for the answer you have chosen. Be sure to fill in the circle completely.

1 _____ was one good reason for changing the weak national government set up by the Articles of Confederation.
- Ⓐ The Northwest Ordinance
- Ⓑ The way Congress moved around
- Ⓒ Shays's Rebellion
- Ⓓ The idea of James Madison

2 The Great Compromise established—
- Ⓕ how enslaved African Americans would be counted.
- Ⓖ who had the right to tax.
- Ⓗ the balance between state and federal government.
- Ⓙ how states would be represented in Congress.

3 A President who does not perform the duties of the office can be—
- Ⓐ impeached by Congress.
- Ⓑ forced to leave town.
- Ⓒ tried before the Supreme Court.
- Ⓓ sent to a foreign country.

4 The Bill of Rights was influenced by the—
- Ⓕ Spanish constitution.
- Ⓖ British Magna Carta.
- Ⓗ Italian Bill of Rights.
- Ⓙ French political practice.

5 George Washington set an example for future Presidents by—
- Ⓐ riding a white horse.
- Ⓑ placing his friends in government positions.
- Ⓒ serving only two elected terms.
- Ⓓ naming the person to be the next President.

Use after reading Chapter 10, pages 344–379.

The Louisiana Purchase

Directions Read each numbered item below. Fill in each blank with the name of the person or persons connected to the description. Use names from the Word Bank. You may use a name more than once.

Sacagawea	Thomas Jefferson	Meriwether Lewis	Zebulon Pike
York	William Clark	Napoleon Bonaparte	

1 hoped to revive French power in North America

Napoleon Bonaparte _____

2 wanted the United States to have a port on the lower Mississippi River

Thomas Jefferson _____

3 needed money to fight a war Napoleon Bonaparte _____

4 leaders of the Corps of Discovery Meriwether Lewis and William Clark _____

5 African American who helped the Corps of Discovery by hunting and fishing

York _____

6 helped the Corps of Discovery by guiding them through the land of the

Shoshones Sacagawea _____

7 explored the southwestern portion of the Louisiana Purchase

Zebulon Pike _____

The War of 1812

Directions Look at the time line below. Match the events with the correct date on the time line. Place the letter of the correct event in the blank provided.

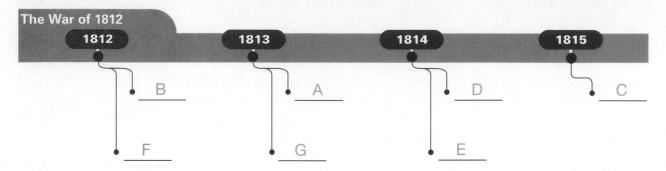

The War of 1812

| 1812 | 1813 | 1814 | 1815 |

B ___   A ___   D ___   C ___

F ___   G ___   E ___

A. Battle of Lake Erie

B. United States declares war against Britain

C. Battle of New Orleans

D. British burn Washington, D.C.

E. Francis Scott Key writes "The Defense of Fort McHenry"

F. The warship *Constitution* defeats the British ship *Guerriére*.

G. Battle of the Thames

(continued)

Use after reading Chapter 11, Lesson 2, pages 389–394.

Name _____ Date _____

Directions **Answer the questions below.**

1 Give two reasons that the United States declared war on Britain.

The British in Canada supplied Native

Americans with guns and impressed

United States sailors.

_____

2 What United States senator believed that the United States should "take the whole

continent"? Henry Clay _____

3 What was the nickname of the warship *Constitution*? Old Ironsides _____

4 What Shawnee Indian leader was killed at the Battle of the Thames?

Tecumseh _____

5 What action did Dolley Madison take before leaving the White House?

She saved important government papers and a portrait of George Washington.

_____

6 What did Francis Scott Key do after seeing the battle at Fort McHenry?

He wrote the poem that later became known as "The Star-Spangled Banner."

_____

7 What years came to be known as the Era of Good Feelings?

1817–1825 _____

8 Why was the Battle of New Orleans unnecessary? A peace treaty between the

British and the Americans had been signed two weeks before, on

December 24, 1814.

_____

© Harcourt

The Age of Jackson

Directions Read the paragraph below. Fill in the graphic organizer to show why the United States Supreme Court said the Cherokees could keep their land. Then answer the questions that follow.

United States Supreme Court Chief Justice John Marshall wrote the opinion of the Court in the case of *Worcester* v. *Georgia*. Marshall referred to Britain's past treaties with the Cherokee. He said the Cherokee had honored the treaties. That proved that the Cherokee were a nation able to govern themselves. He also argued that the laws of Georgia had no power over the Cherokee nation people because they were a "distinct community." Finally, Marshall said that the Native Americans had previous possession of the land. It was theirs. Unfortunately, President Andrew Jackson refused to accept the ruling. He said, "John Marshall has made his decision; now let him enforce it." Jackson then ordered federal troops to remove the Native Americans and take the land.

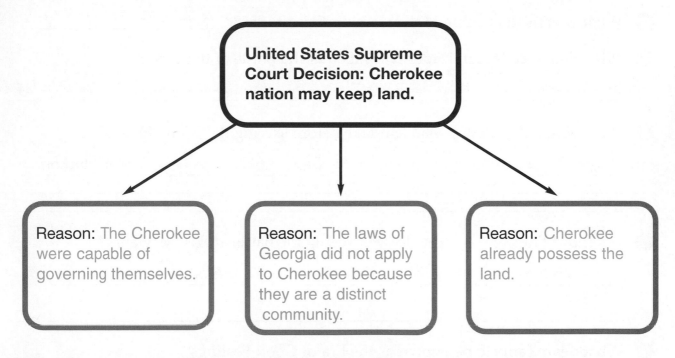

United States Supreme Court Decision: Cherokee nation may keep land.

Reason: The Cherokee were capable of governing themselves.

Reason: The laws of Georgia did not apply to Cherokee because they are a distinct community.

Reason: Cherokee already possess the land.

1 Who was John Marshall? a United States Supreme Court Chief Justice

2 What did President Andrew Jackson say about Marshall's decision?

"John Marshall has made his decision; now let him enforce it."

_____

3 What did Jackson then do? President Jackson ordered federal troops to remove

the Native Americans and take their land.

Use after reading Chapter 11, Lesson 3, pages 395–399.

From Ocean to Ocean

Directions **Fill in the blanks in the paragraph below, using terms from the Word Bank.**

| Mormons | gold rush | dictator | forty-niners |
| Oregon | Cession | manifest destiny | |

In the early 1800s many people began to believe that the United States should

stretch from the Atlantic Ocean to the Pacific Ocean. This idea was known as

_____manifest destiny_____. In time, this goal seemed possible. In 1834

when General Santa Anna took over the Mexican government and made himself

_____dictator_____, Texas settlers were alarmed. After battles at the

Alamo and San Jacinto, the settlers defeated Santa Anna and Texas became an

independent republic. Several years later, Mexico and the United States again clashed

over the Texas border. Mexico agreed to give up its claims in what was called the

Mexican _____Cession_____. In addition, some people went west in

search of religious freedom. The _____Mormons_____ settled in Utah

after being driven from Illinois. Marcus and Narcissa Whitman went to the

_____Oregon_____ Territory to set up missions. Finally, when gold

was discovered in California, a _____gold rush_____ began.

Those who went called themselves _____forty-niners_____ because

many settlers moved there in 1849.

MAP AND GLOBE SKILLS
Identifying Changing Borders

Directions Use the map below to answer the questions that follow.

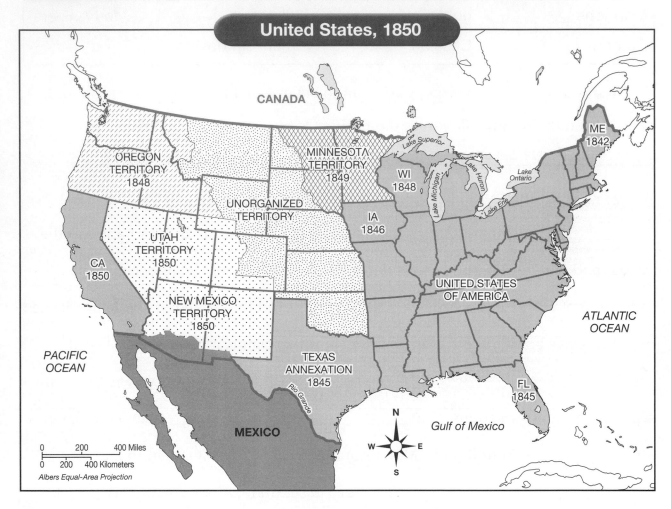

United States, 1850

1 In what year did the United States gain control of the Utah Territory? 1850 _____

2 What state was the farthest west in 1850? California _____

3 What river eventually became the border between Mexico and the United States?

Rio Grande _____

4 By 1850 had the idea of manifest destiny been achieved? Explain.

Yes; Possible answer: By 1850 the United States had control of the Oregon

Territory and had gained California as a state. The United States now stretched

from the Atlantic to the Pacific Ocean.

© Harcourt

An Industrial Revolution

Directions **Tell how each invention listed below played a part in the Industrial Revolution. Write your answers on the blanks provided.** Students' answers will vary; possible answers are given.

1 The steam engine The steam engine was used in both boats and trains. It reduced the time and cost of travel and shipping.

2 Cotton mills The machines to spin thread and weave cloth cut the time needed to make fabric. Mills were the first examples of large-scale manufacturing in the United States. People began working in factories instead of at home.

3 Interchangeable parts This made mass production possible. The supply of manufactured goods increased.

4 Cotton gin The cotton gin removed seeds from cotton faster than people could. This allowed cotton to be cleaned and prepared for market in less time.

5 Mechanical reaper The reaper allowed farmers to harvest as much wheat in one day as they could in two weeks using hand tools.

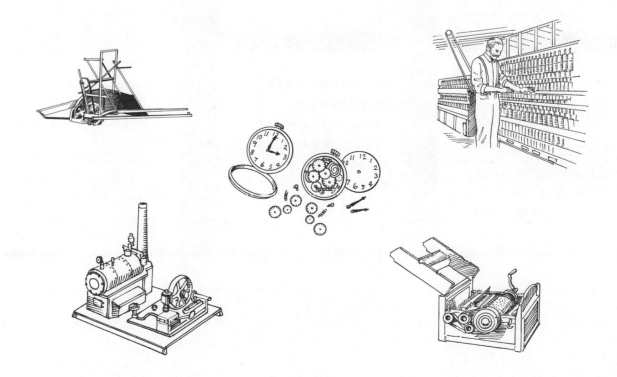

© Harcourt

Use after reading Chapter 11, Lesson 5, pages 412–419.

America and the Industrial Revolution

Directions Complete this graphic organizer by drawing conclusions about the Industrial Revolution.

WHAT YOU KNOW	NEW FACTS	CONCLUSION
Student answers will vary. Sample answer: At the time, most Americans had never been anywhere outside of the United States.	Life was often difficult for Americans, especially those who chose to settle in unexplored lands.	The Industrial Revolution made the lives of most Americans much easier, improving the ways many people lived, traveled, and worked.
Student answers will vary. Sample answer: At one time, Americans did most farming work by hand.	With new inventions like the reaper, wheat that once took two weeks to cut could now be cut in one day.	
Student answers will vary. Sample answer: Traveling in the United States was once very difficult and took a great deal of time.	By the mid-1800s more than 88 thousand miles of road and 9 thousand miles of rail had been built in the United States.	

Use after reading Chapter 11, pages 383–419.

11 Test Preparation

Directions Read each question and choose the best answer. Then fill in the circle for the answer you have chosen. Be sure to fill in the circle completely.

1 Napoleon was willing to sell Louisiana because—
- Ⓐ he knew he was too far away to control it.
- Ⓑ he had no use for the land.
- Ⓒ he needed money to fight a war.
- Ⓓ he was persuaded by Jefferson's representatives.

2 The years from 1817 to 1825 are called—
- Ⓕ the Age of Jackson.
- Ⓖ manifest destiny.
- Ⓗ the Monroe Doctrine.
- Ⓙ the Era of Good Feelings.

3 All of the following are reasons for Andrew Jackson's election *except* that—
- Ⓐ he was a war hero.
- Ⓑ he had lots of money.
- Ⓒ for the first time all white men could vote.
- Ⓓ he was considered a common man.

4 During the 1850s, settlers moving west followed the—
- Ⓕ Erie Canal.
- Ⓖ Oregon Trail.
- Ⓗ Royal Road.
- Ⓙ Northwest Passage.

5 *Tom Thumb* proved that—
- Ⓐ steam-powered railroad engines were faster than horses.
- Ⓑ locomotives were undependable.
- Ⓒ steam-powered railroad cars had better pulling power than horses.
- Ⓓ trains needed much improvement to be practical.

© Harcourt

Use after reading Chapter 11, pages 382–421.

Expansion and Change

Directions Each sentence below tells a story about Canada's growth. Circle the word or phrase that correctly completes each sentence.

1 Alexander Mackenzie led the first expedition across Canada's western lands for the (North West Company / Hudson's Bay Company).

2 (Voyageurs / Métis) were French-Canadian trappers who explored Canadian rivers and lakes in search of furs to trade.

3 (John A. Macdonald / Selkirk) bought a large area of land along the Red River and settled thousands of Scottish farmers in a new colony.

4 (John A. Macdonald / Sir Hugh Allan) was Canada's first national leader, whose task was to unite the diverse people of Canada.

5 The British, hoping that settlements would strengthen their western land claims, founded (Toronto / Vancouver) in 1865.

6 John A. Macdonald's government chose a company headed by (Sir Hugh Allan / Wilfrid Laurier) to build part of a railroad in British Columbia.

7 In 1885, Canadians linked the eastern and western provinces with the completion of a (railroad / highway).

8 Between 1896 and 1911 more than two million immigrants settled in large cities, such as Toronto, Winnipeg, and (Montreal / Red River).

© Harcourt

Use after reading Unit 5, pages U5-1 to U5-15.

Name _____ Date _____

Directions Mexico lost large amounts of land throughout its history. Follow the instructions below to locate and name some important places in Mexican history.

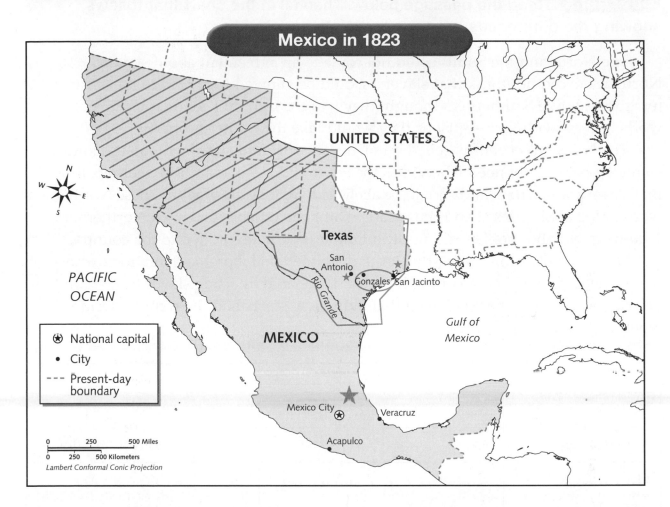

Mexico in 1823

1. Draw a circle around the site of the first battle of the Texas Revolution. What is the name of this town? Gonzales

2. Draw stars on two important battle sites of the Texas Revolution. What are the names of those sites? San Antonio and San Jacinto

3. Draw a border around the land that Mexico lost when Texas declared its independence. Students should draw a border around this area of land.

4. Draw a large star next to the place where the last battle of the Mexican War was fought. Where did this battle take place? Mexico City

5. Add shading on the land granted to the United States by the Mexican Cession and the Gadsden Purchase. Students should shade this area of land.

Regional Disagreements

Directions Read the passage below. Then fill in the chart that follows, showing the differences between the North and South.

The North and the South could not come to an agreement about slavery. Northerners did not think that slavery should be allowed to spread to the western territories, while Southerners thought they had the right to take their enslaved workers west with them—just as they would take their other property.

The Northern economy relied on manufacturing and shipping, not agriculture, so the North did not need laborers as the South did. Also, many Northerners thought that slavery was wrong and should be abolished, or done away with. Those Northerners were called abolitionists, and they wanted all people to be free. Even Northerners who were not abolitionists did not want more slave states added to the country.

However, the economy of the South depended on laborers. Plantation owners were able to harvest more cotton, indigo, and tobacco by using slaves to work in the fields. Those Southerners believed that individual states had the right to decide whether people could have slaves.

	North	South
Economy based on	manufacturing and shipping	farming
Viewed slavery as	wrong	a necessity to work the fields
Ideas about extending slavery	No more slave states should come into the nation.	States had the right to decide whether people could own slaves.

Directions Use the passage and chart above to answer the questions.

1 What were Northerners called who did not agree with slavery? Why were they called that? abolitionists; the word *abolition* means "the act of doing away with," so abolitionists wanted to do away with slavery.

2 Where did most Northerners believe slavery should not be allowed to spread? the western territories

Use after reading Chapter 12, Lesson 1, pages 436–441.

© Harcourt

CITIZENSHIP SKILLS

Identify Frame of Reference

Directions Read the material below and then answer the questions.

Henry Clay

When Missouri asked to be a state in 1819, Henry Clay was a congress member from Kentucky. Although Clay owned slaves, he did not want slavery to divide the country. He worked very hard to find a solution that would make both the North and the South happy. While other members of Congress were arguing for their region of the country, Clay said, "I know no South, no North, no East, no West, to which I owe any allegiance [loyalty]." His solution was called the Missouri Compromise.

John Quincy Adams

John Quincy Adams, a Northerner, was the secretary of state at the time. Adams kept a diary, and in February 1820 he wrote about what he thought the future might bring, ". . . if the dissolution [breaking apart] of the Union should result from the slave question, it is as obvious as anything. . . that it must shortly afterwards be followed by the universal emancipation [freeing] of the slaves. . ."

1 What viewpoint did Henry Clay have about the Union? How do you know?

Clay thought that the Union was more important than any one region of the

country. He said he was not loyal to any one section of the country.

_____

2 What did John Quincy Adams think would happen if the Union broke apart?

Shortly afterwards, all slaves would be freed.

Name _____ Date _____

Slavery and Freedom

Directions On the blanks provided, write the word or name that best completes each sentence. Some letters in your answers will have numbers under them. Write these letters in the appropriate boxes below, and you will find the name of the most famous conductor of the Underground Railroad.

1 A man named <u>N a t</u> <u>T u r n e r</u> led the first slave rebellion.

                          7

2 Something done in secret is done <u>u n d e r g r o u n d</u>.

                                   3

3 A person who is running away is a <u>f u g i t i v e</u>.

                                9

4 To act against slavery is to <u>r e s i s t</u> it.

                          4

5 The Virginia legislature debated the <u>e m a n c i p a t i o n</u>, or freeing, of slaves.

                             11   2

6 Sets of laws, known as slave <u>c o d e s</u>, ruled the lives of slaves.

                                6

7 Harriet Beecher Stowe wrote a book titled <u>U n c l e</u> <u>T o m's</u> <u>C a b i n</u>.

                               8   13

8 The newspaper *Freedom's Journal* called for <u>e q u a l i t y</u>, or equal rights for all people.

                               12

9 Someone who wanted to end slavery was called an <u>a b o l i t i o n i s t</u>.

                                10   5

10 A former slave named <u>S o j o u r n e r</u> <u>T r u t h</u> traveled the country to speak out against slavery.

                                       1

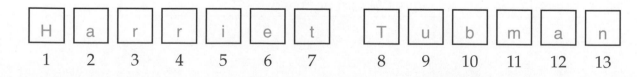

H	a	r	r	i	e	t		T	u	b	m	a	n
1	2	3	4	5	6	7		8	9	10	11	12	13

© Harcourt

Use after reading Chapter 12, Lesson 2, pages 444–449.

The Union Breaks Apart

Directions Read the passage below. Then read each statement that follows. If the statement is true, write *T* in the blank. If the statement is false, write *F* in the blank.

Abraham Lincoln had barely a year of formal schooling, but he learned to read and write. He was very intelligent and read everything he could. Growing up, Lincoln had many jobs such as a rail-splitter, riverboat man, store clerk, and postmaster. After studying very hard on his own, he finally became a lawyer.

About five years later, in 1842, Abe Lincoln married Mary Todd. Soon after, they purchased a home in Springfield, Illinois. The Lincolns had four sons, but only one lived past the age of 19.

In 1846, Lincoln was elected to the United States Congress, where he served one term in the House of Representatives. Fourteen years later, he was elected President of the United States. Lincoln is the only President to own a patent for an invention. In 1849 he patented a device for lifting boats up over shallow places in rivers. Lincoln was also presented with several honorary degrees during the time of the Civil War.

As respected and honored as President Lincoln was, Mrs. Lincoln was not very popular in Washington. She came from a Southern family, and four of her brothers were in the Confederate army. Some people feared Mary Lincoln was a Confederate spy.

___T___ **1** The Lincolns had four children.

___F___ **2** Mrs. Lincoln was well liked in Washington.

___T___ **3** Mrs. Lincoln had brothers in the Confederate army.

___F___ **4** Lincoln never owned a home of his own.

___T___ **5** Lincoln received several honorary degrees.

___F___ **6** Many presidents had inventions that they patented.

___F___ **7** Lincoln went to school for many years.

___F___ **8** Lincoln was elected to the United States Senate.

© Harcourt

Use after reading Chapter 12, Lesson 3, pages 450–455.

MAP AND GLOBE SKILLS

Compare Maps with Different Scales

Directions Look at the maps below, and then answer the questions on the facing page.

Map A: The Missouri Compromise, 1820

UNORGANIZED TERRITORY

MICHIGAN TERRITORY

MAINE

VT

NH

NEW YORK

MA

CT

RI

PENNSYLVANIA

NJ

INDIANA   OHIO

MD   DE

ILLINOIS

VIRGINIA

MISSOURI COMPROMISE LINE

MISSOURI

KENTUCKY

NORTH CAROLINA

TENNESSEE

SOUTH CAROLINA

ATLANTIC OCEAN

ARKANSAS TERRITORY

ALABAMA   GEORGIA

MISSISSIPPI

LOUISIANA

FLORIDA TERRITORY

Gulf of Mexico

Free state
Free territory
Admitted as a free state
Slave state
Slave territory
Admitted as a slave state
Missouri Compromise line
Present-day border

0 100 200 Miles
0 100 200 Kilometers

N E S W

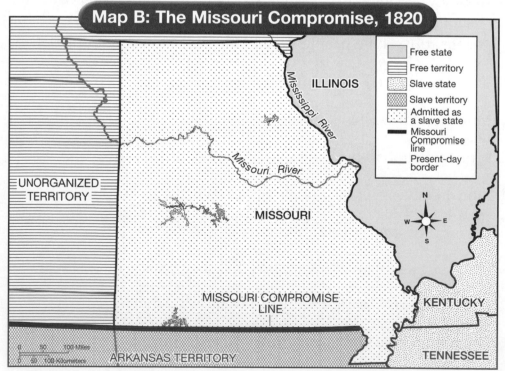

Map B: The Missouri Compromise, 1820

UNORGANIZED TERRITORY

ILLINOIS

Mississippi River

Missouri River

MISSOURI

Free state
Free territory
Slave state
Slave territory
Admitted as a slave state
Missouri Compromise line
Present-day border

N E S W

MISSOURI COMPROMISE LINE

KENTUCKY

0 50 100 Miles
0 50 100 Kilometers

ARKANSAS TERRITORY

TENNESSEE

(continued)

Use after reading Chapter 12, Skill Lesson, pages 456–457.

Name _____ Date _____

1 Which map would be used to compare the size of Missouri to the size of Maine?

Map A

2 Which map would be used to determine the length of the border between

Missouri and Kentucky? Map B

3 How many slave states were there at the time of the Missouri Compromise?

11

4 Was there more free territory or slave territory reserved?

free territory

5 Which state entered the Union at the same time as Missouri?

Maine

6 How many free states were there at the time of the Missouri Compromise?

11

Directions **Compare the two maps. Write *A* in the answer blank if Map A is more useful, and *B* if Map B is more useful.**

___B___ **7** Determine the length of the part of the Mississippi River that forms a Missouri border.

___A___ **8** Determine whether the free or slave states had the largest land area.

___B___ **9** Determine the length of the part of the Missouri River that flows from the eastern border to the western border of Missouri.

___A___ **10** Determine the number of miles of border separating the free states and the slave states.

Use after reading Chapter 12, Skill Lesson, pages 456–457.

Civil War

Directions In the box provided, write a brief paragraph to explain why each item on the left was important to the Civil War. Student responses will vary. Possible responses are given.

EVENT   **IMPORTANT BECAUSE**

The Battle of Bull Run

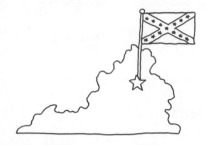

The Battle of Bull Run was the first major battle fought between the Union and Confederacy. The Confederates won the battle, proving to the Northerners that the South was more powerful than they thought.

Anaconda Plan

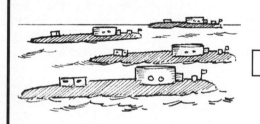

The purpose of the Union plan was to win control of the Mississippi River and blockade Confederate ports so that the South could not ship its cotton or bring in cash crops, it would not have money to buy supplies for its army.

The Battle of Antietam

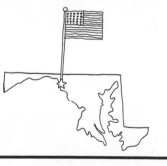

Although the fighting at Antietam ended in nearly a tie, as a result of the battle President Lincoln announced his decision to issue an order freeing the slaves in areas that were still fighting against the Union.

The Emancipation Proclamation

The presidential order said that all slaves living in those parts of the South still fighting against the Union would be freed. The Emancipation Proclamation also hurt the South's chances of getting help from Britain and France.

© Harcourt

The Road to Union Victory

Directions Place the Civil War events in chronological order by numbering the dates on the time line.

1 Much of Atlanta burns to the ground after being captured by the Union army.

2 The Confederate army wins the Battle of Chancellorsville, and heads north towards Gettysburg.

3 The Union victory at the Battle of Gettysburg cripples the Confederate army.

4 General Robert E. Lee surrenders at Appomattox Court House, Virginia.

5 Lincoln gives the Gettysburg Address to inspire the nation and Union soldiers.

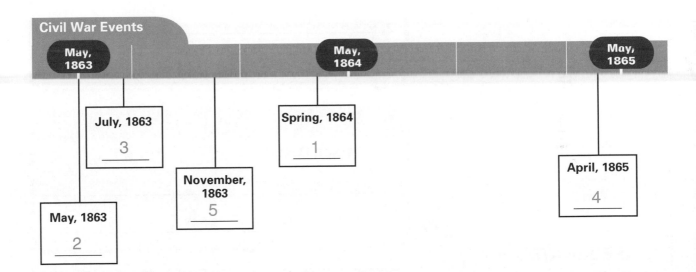

Important Leaders and Battles of the Civil War

Directions Complete this graphic organizer by categorizing important leaders and battles of the Civil War.

IMPORTANT LEADERS
1. **Abraham Lincoln**
2. Ulysses S. Grant
3. William Tecumseh Sherman

UNION ARMY

IMPORTANT VICTORIES
1. **Battle of Gettysburg**
2. Battle of Vicksburg
3. Sherman's capture of Atlanta

IMPORTANT LEADERS
1. **Jefferson Davis**
2. Robert E. Lee
3. Thomas "Stonewall" Jackson

CONFEDERATE ARMY

IMPORTANT VICTORIES
1. **Victory at Fort Sumter**
2. Battle of Bull Run
3. Battle of Chancellorsville

Use after reading Chapter 12, pages 435–471.

Name _____ Date _____

12 Test Preparation

Directions Read each question and choose the best answer. Then fill in the circle for the answer you have chosen. Be sure to fill in the circle completely.

1 Who was one of the men who persuaded Congress to accept the Missouri Compromise?
ⓐ John Calhoun
ⓑ Daniel Webster
ⓒ Henry Clay
ⓓ Abraham Lincoln

2 Who defended the rights of both slaves and women?
ⓕ Elizabeth Cady Stanton
ⓖ Harriet Beecher Stowe
ⓗ Clara Barton
ⓙ Mary Todd Lincoln

3 Abraham Lincoln became well known through his debates with—
ⓐ Henry Clay.
ⓑ Stephen Douglas.
ⓒ Jefferson Davis.
ⓓ Major Robert Anderson.

4 The Union strategy to win the war by weakening the South was called the—
ⓕ Join or Die Plan.
ⓖ slash and burn policy.
ⓗ King Cotton policy.
ⓙ Anaconda Plan.

5 How did Abraham Lincoln honor the dead at Gettysburg?
ⓐ He set up a memorial fund.
ⓑ He had a monument built at the cemetery.
ⓒ He gave a speech at the cemetery.
ⓓ He sent the Vice President to the battlefield.

Use after reading Chapter 12, pages 436–471.

Name _____   Date _____

Reconstruction

Directions Read the time line below of events surrounding Reconstruction.
Then answer the questions that follow.

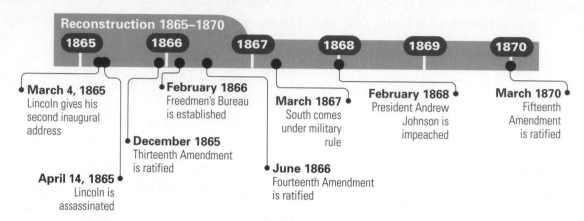

1 Was the Thirteenth Amendment ratified before or after President Lincoln gave

his second inaugural address? after _____

2 What happened to President Abraham Lincoln on April 14, 1865?

He was assassinated. _____

_____

3 About how many years passed between President Lincoln's assassination and

President Johnson's impeachment? three _____

4 What two events shown on the time line both happened in the month of

February? The Freedmen's Bureau was established and President Johnson

was impeached. _____

5 Was the Freedmen's Bureau established before or after the South came under

military rule? before _____

_____

6 How many constitutional amendments were passed between 1865 and 1870?

three _____

Use after reading Chapter 13, Lesson 1, pages 476–480.

© Harcourt

The South After the War

Directions Match each vocabulary word with its definition. Then use the vocabulary words to fill in the blanks of the sentences below.

___D___ **1** former slaves

___B___ **2** government agency

___F___ **3** the practice of paying farm workers in harvested crops

___E___ **4** Northerners who went South during Reconstruction

___C___ **5** a method of voting in which no one knows for whom you voted

___A___ **6** separation of people based on race

A. segregation

B. bureau

C. secret ballot

D. freedmen

E. carpetbaggers

F. sharecropping

7 The _____secret ballot_____ is one of the most important parts of a fair election.

8 There are still many _____bureaus_____ in the United States government.

9 Life was hard for the _____freedmen_____ after the Civil War since few of them had enough money to buy their own land.

10 _____carpetbaggers_____ were given their name because of the suitcases many of them used to carry their belongings.

11 The practice of _____segregation_____ kept people apart in most public places.

12 Under the _____sharecropping_____ system most farmworkers found it difficult to make a living.

© Harcourt

Use after reading Chapter 13, Lesson 2, pages 481–485.

Name _____ Date _____

Settling the Last Frontier

Directions Study the map below.

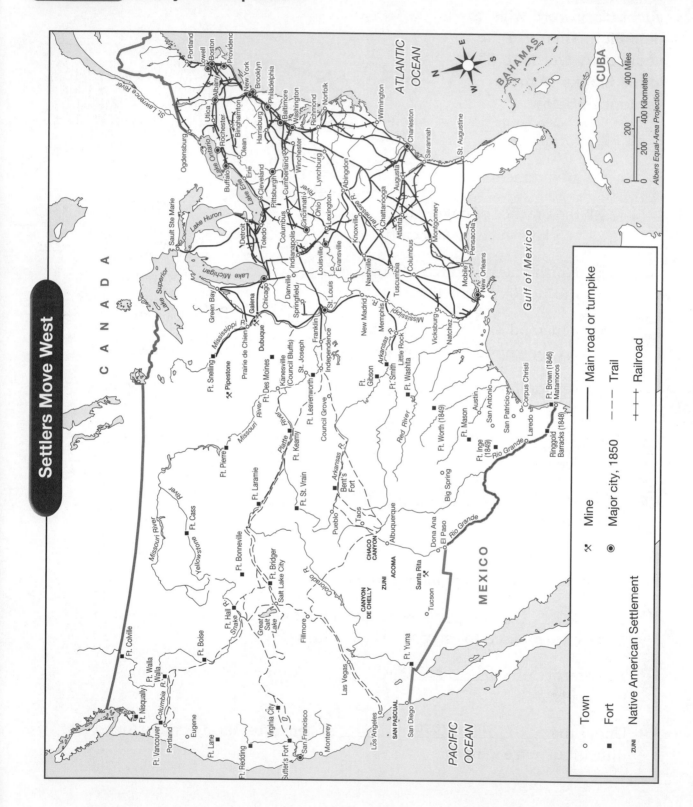

(continued)

Use after reading Chapter 13, Lesson 3, pages 486–491.

Name _____ Date _____

Directions Use the map and key on the preceding page to help you answer the questions. Write your answers in the blanks provided.

1 In what part of the country were most railroads located?

East

2 What Texas fort was the farthest west? Ft. Inge

3 In what parts of the country were most forts located? in the West and Midwest

_____

4 Could you travel by railroad from St. Louis, Missouri, to Salt Lake City?

no

5 How might you travel from Norfolk, Virginia, to Wilmington, North Carolina?

railroad or main road

6 Find the area that represents your state on the map. How settled was it? What might life have been like for the settlers who lived there?

Answers will vary.

_____

_____

_____

_____

© Harcourt

CHART AND GRAPH SKILLS
Use a Climograph

Directions Look at the climograph of Austin, Texas, below. Then answer the questions on the blanks provided.

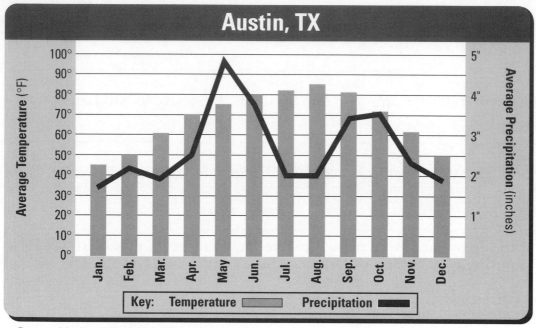

Source: National Drought Mitigation Center

(continued)

Use after reading Chapter 13, Skill Lesson, pages 492–493.

Name _____ Date _____

1 What is the average temperature in Austin in July? about 82 degrees F

2 What is the average precipitation in October? about 3.5 inches

3 Which three months are the driest? January, March, December

4 Which month is the coolest month? January

5 Which month is the warmest month? August

6 Which month gets the most precipitation? May

7 What do you observe about the months of July and August?

They are nearly the same in both average temperature and rainfall.

8 If you were driving cattle, what months do you think would be hardest on

people and cattle? What hardships might you face during the drive?

Answers will vary but may include the wettest months, driest months, hottest

months, and coldest months. Hardships may include unexpected rainstorms,

drought, and extreme heat or cold.

_____

Use after reading Chapter 13, Skill Lesson, pages 492–493.

The Rise of New Industries

Directions **Read the passages below, and answer the questions that follow.**

In the 1800s the United States government made land grants to several railroad companies. More than 130 million acres were given to the Union Pacific, the Santa Fe, the Central and Southern Pacific, and the Northern Pacific railroads. In addition, western states gave the railroads 49 million acres. These land grants allowed the railroad industry to open new markets in the West for goods produced in the East.

One effect of the railroad boom was the need for stronger track. When the railroads were first built, the rails were made of iron. With the arrival of bigger and faster locomotives, however, these iron rails were not strong enough to withstand the weight of the new trains. A man named Henry Bessemer invented a way to make steel tracks strong enough for the larger locomotives. As a result, many companies were able to ship their products throughout the United States at a faster pace.

One company that used the new, faster trains to its advantage was Standard Oil. Founded by John D. Rockefeller in 1867, Standard Oil used the trains to ship oil all over the country. By 1882 Standard Oil controlled almost all of the oil refining and distribution in the United States.

1 Where did the railroad companies get the land on which they built the lines? The United States government and western states made land grants.

2 What effect did replacing iron rails with steel rails have on how United States companies could ship their products? Many United States companies could now ship their products at a faster pace.

3 What company did John D. Rockefeller found in 1867? Standard Oil

4 What role do you think the railroads played in the growth of Standard Oil? Standard Oil used the railroads to ship oil all over the United States. As a result, by 1882, the company controlled most of the oil distribution in the United States.

A Changing People

Directions Read the passage below and answer the questions that follow.

Irving Berlin's father was a cantor, a person who sings at religious services in Jewish synagogues. Perhaps it was his father's music that caused Berlin to be interested in writing songs. When he was in the Army during World War I, Berlin wrote a musical show. He later won both the United States Army's Award of Merit and a congressional medal for his songs. One of his most popular songs is "God Bless America."

Although Sophia Alice Callahan lived to be only 26 years old, she wrote an important novel. *Wynema: A Child of the Forest* is thought to be the first novel written by a Native American woman. Callahan's father was one-eighth Creek Indian. The novel has two major characters, Wynema and a Methodist teacher named Genevieve, who try to overcome prejudice against both Indians and women in the late nineteenth century.

Hiram Fong graduated from Harvard Law School before he returned to his native Hawaii to practice law. Hawaii at that time was still a territory. Fong served in the territorial legislature from 1938 to 1954. When Hawaii became a state, he was elected to the United States Senate. He served in the Senate from 1959 until 1977.

African American artist Jacob Lawrence did a 63-painting series on the lives of Harriet Tubman and Frederick Douglass. He studied painting in the Harlem section of New York City. During the depression, Lawrence worked for a federal project. This gave him enough money to be able to paint *Migration*, a series of 60 panels showing the movement of African Americans from the South to the North.

1 Explain what all the people in the passage have in common.

All were members of minority groups. Berlin was Jewish, Callahan was a

Native American woman, Fong was Asian, and Lawrence was African American.

2 Who might have influenced Irving Berlin's interest in music?

his father, who was a cantor

3 How did Hiram Fong serve his homeland? He was part of the territorial legislature

and a member of the Senate after Hawaii became a state.

4 What two series of paintings were created by Jacob Lawrence?

a series on Harriet Tubman and Frederick Douglass and a series titled *Migration*,

showing the movement of African Americans from the South to the North

© Harcourt

Abraham Lincoln and Reconstruction

Directions Complete this graphic organizer by describing different points of view about Reconstruction.

WHO SAID IT	WHAT WAS SAID	WHY IT WAS SAID	POINT OF VIEW
Abraham Lincoln	"With malice toward none, with charity for all, with firmness in the right as God gives us to see the right, let us strive on to finish the work we are in, to bind up the nation's wounds…"	Because the country had been torn apart by the Civil War	Lincoln believed the South should not be punished for the Civil War and that the country should be brought back together peacefully and quickly.

WHO SAID IT	WHAT WAS SAID	WHY IT WAS SAID	POINT OF VIEW
Mary Chesnut	"Lincoln—old Abe Lincoln—killed… I know this foul murder will bring down miseries on us."	In response to Abraham Lincoln's assassination	Chesnut feared that, with the President gone, the South would now be held responsible for the Civil War and Lincoln's murder.

Use after reading Chapter 13, pages 475–507.

Test Preparation

Directions Read each question and choose the best answer. Then fill in the circle for the answer you have chosen. Be sure to fill in the circle completely.

1 Which of the following was **not** a condition for a Southern state's readmission to the Union?

Ⓐ rewriting the state's constitution

Ⓑ giving slaves some of the land

Ⓒ ratifying the Thirteenth Amendment

Ⓓ ratifying the Fifteenth Amendment

2 The most important work of the Freedmen's Bureau was—

Ⓕ education.

Ⓖ running the courts.

Ⓗ helping people farm.

Ⓙ rebuilding homes.

3 Which of the following was **not** a problem for homesteaders?

Ⓐ drought

Ⓑ range wars

Ⓒ bitter cold and snow

Ⓓ land costs

4 The last spike of the transcontinental railroad was driven at—

Ⓕ Spokane, Washington.

Ⓖ Promontory, Utah.

Ⓗ Erie, Pennsylvania.

Ⓙ St. Louis, Missouri.

5 The term "new immigration" refers to—

Ⓐ people coming from Britain, Germany, and Ireland.

Ⓑ African Americans moving north.

Ⓒ people coming from Italy, Russia, and Greece.

Ⓓ people coming from South America.

Regional Diversity

Directions Canada has five economic regions and many industries. Write the letter of each industry listed below in the correct region or regions. You may use your textbook to help you match the industries with the regions.

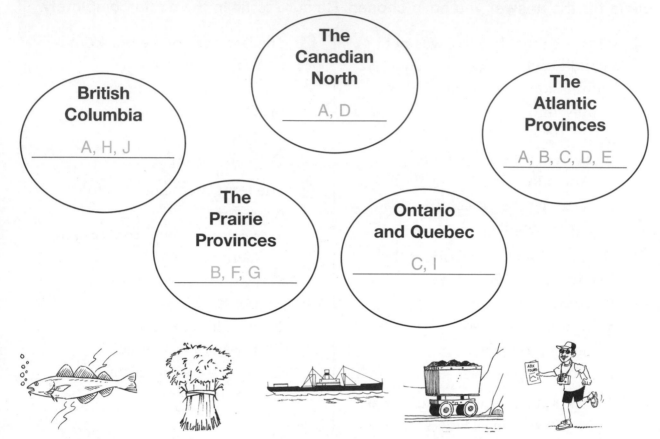

British Columbia

A, H, J

The Canadian North

A, D

The Atlantic Provinces

A, B, C, D, E

The Prairie Provinces

B, F, G

Ontario and Quebec

C, I

A. cod fishing **B.** farming **C.** shipping **D.** mining **E.** tourism

F. oil and natural gas drilling **G.** cattle ranching **H.** logging **I.** iron and steel production **J.** hydroelectric power

© Harcourt

Name _____ Date _____

Directions The passages below describe some of Mexico's social and economic conflicts. Read each passage and summarize the main idea.

1 Three out of every four Mexicans live in a city or town. Some of the largest cities in Mexico are in the northern states of Nuevo León and Baja California Norte. When the government decided to promote manufacturing there, many factories were built. People moved to the northern states in search of work. As a result, the cities there have grown faster than other cities in Mexico.

The promotion of manufacturing caused many Mexicans to move to northern

Mexican cities in search of work.

2 Until the 1900s most of the fertile land in Mexico was owned by a small number of landowners. The majority of Mexicans owned small farms that grew poor crops. Other farmers had no land at all. The poor farmers pushed for land reform, and the Constitution of 1917 met their demands. The new constitution broke up large estates and distributed land to the poor farmers.

Most Mexicans had little or no farmland until the Constitution of 1917 broke up

large estates and distributed the land.

3 Today, many poor farmers in the state of Oaxaca and on the Yucatán Peninsula cannot earn a living by farming. Many farmers have poor land on which few crops will grow. Some farmers are selling their farms to large landowners. Others simply leave their fields and move to Mexican or American cities.

Many Mexican farmers, unable to earn a living by farming, sell their land or leave

their farms.

4 On New Year's Eve in 1993, a revolt began in the state of Chiapas. A group of 2,000 Mayan peasants took control of several towns. They claimed that the Mexican government's economic policies left them poor. The Mayans also demanded more land and self-rule for all of Mexico's indigenous people.

Mayan peasants in the state of Chiapas revolted because they wanted more land,

self-rule, and an end to the economic policies that left indigenous people poor.

© Harcourt

Building an American Empire

Directions Use the information below to complete the chart.

- Americans set up a republic in 1893. The United States annexes the territory in 1898.

- Source of fish, timber, coal, copper, and gold

- Secretary of State William Seward buys the land from Russia in 1867.

- For producing cattle and sugar

- To link American ports on the Atlantic coast with those on the Pacific coast

- The United States supports a revolution against Colombia. In 1904, the United States begins a major building project.

Territory	How and When Territory Was Added	Reason for Acquiring Territory
Alaska	Secretary of State William Seward buys the land from Russia in 1867.	Source of fish, timber, coal, copper, and gold
Hawaii	Americans set up a republic in 1893. The United States annexes the territory in 1898.	For producing cattle and sugar
Panama Canal Zone	The United States supports a revolution against Colombia. In 1904, the United States begins a major building project.	To link American ports on the Atlantic coast with those on the Pacific coast

(continued)

© Harcourt

Use after reading Chapter 14, Lesson 1, pages 524–529.

Name _____ Date _____

Directions Use the information from the table on the previous page and the map below to write a paragraph to convince someone that Alaska, Hawaii, or the Panama Canal Zone should be added to the United States.

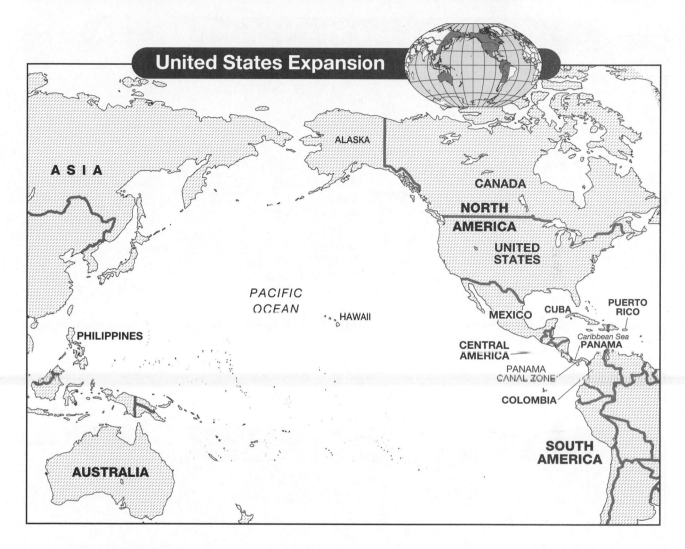

Students' arguments should include the reasons from the chart on the facing page.

For Hawaii students also might mention that the islands provide a useful American

outpost in the Pacific, halfway between the continental United States and the

Philippines. For the Panama Canal Zone, students also might mention that the

canal dramatically shortens the ocean journey from the Atlantic coast of the United

States to the Pacific coast.

_____

_____

MAP AND GLOBE SKILLS
Compare Map Projections

Map A: Europe, 1914

Azimuthal Equal Area Projection

Map B: Europe, 1914

Mercator Conformal Projection

© Harcourt

(continued)

Name _____ Date _____

Directions Study the conformal projection and equal-area projection maps.
For each statement below, put a check mark in the column for which the
statement is true. Some statements will be true for both projections. All
statements will be true for at least one projection.

Conformal Projection	Equal-Area Projection	
✓	✓	**1** Shows the nations of Europe in 1914
	✓	**2** Shows the curved feature of Earth
✓		**3** Uses straight lines for all lines of latitude and longitude
✓		**4** Shows all lines of latitude and longitude at right angles to each other
✓	✓	**5** Shows national borders
	✓	**6** Shows most of the Ottoman Empire
✓	✓	**7** Uses a straight line for the prime meridian
✓	✓	**8** Shows directions correctly
✓	✓	**9** Shows parallels *not* intersecting
	✓	**10** Shows correctly the sizes of nations compared with one another
✓		**11** Shows lines of latitude farther apart at the poles
	✓	**12** Uses curved lines to show latitude
✓	✓	**13** Uses straight lines to show longitude
	✓	**14** Shows lines of longitude closer together toward the north pole
✓		**15** Shows all meridians parallel
	✓	**16** Changes the shapes of nations

Progressives and Reform

Directions Identify which group was responsible for making each of the reforms listed in the Word Bank below. Then write each reform in the correct section of the chart.

end boss rule	National Association for the Advancement of Colored People	national parks	Square Deal
Interstate Commerce Commission		National Urban League	support for injured workers
limit child labor		Pure Food and Drug Act	ten-hour workday
merit system	National League of Women Voters	settlement houses	women's suffrage
			Wisconsin Idea

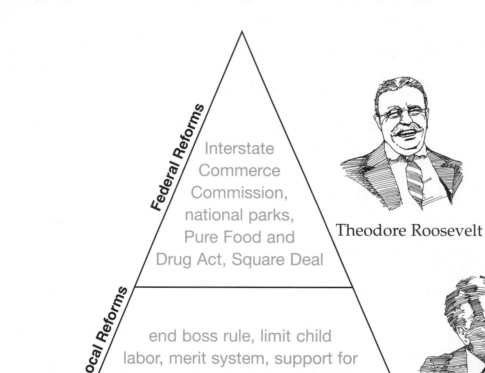

Federal Reforms

Interstate Commerce Commission, national parks, Pure Food and Drug Act, Square Deal

Theodore Roosevelt

State and Local Reforms

end boss rule, limit child labor, merit system, support for injured workers, ten-hour workday, Wisconsin Idea

Robert La Follette

Reforms by Individuals

National Association for the Advancement of Colored People, National League of Women Voters, National Urban League, settlement houses, women's suffrage

W.E.B. DuBois

The Great War

Directions Write a short story about an American family during World War I. Some topics that you may want to feature in your story include worries about German U-boats, concerns about the draft, fighting to make the world "safe for democracy," and thoughts about a family member serving overseas. You may also want to describe how the war has changed the lives of women and African Americans.

_____

_____

_____

_____

_____

_____

_____

_____

_____

_____

_____

_____

_____

_____

© Harcourt

Good Times and Hard Times

Directions Each event listed below occurred either before or after the stock market crash on October 29, 1929. Write the number of each event on the correct side of the time line below.

Before 1929   **After 1929**

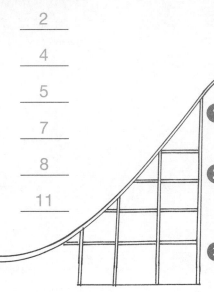

2   1

4   3

5   6

7   9

8   10

11   12

1 The size of the federal government is greatly increased.

2 African American artists, musicians, and writers launch the Harlem Renaissance.

3 Americans elect Franklin Roosevelt for his first term as President.

4 Automobiles become affordable and popular.

5 Charles Lindbergh flies across the Atlantic in the *Spirit of St. Louis.*

6 Congress sets up the Tennessee Valley Authority.

7 For the first time in United States history, more people live in cities than on farms.

8 Moviegoers see the first "talkies."

9 President Roosevelt announces the New Deal.

10 The number of United States commercial radio stations tops 800.

11 Jazz becomes a popular form of music.

12 American farmers are hurt by low crop prices.

Use after reading Chapter 14, Lesson 4, pages 542–549.

The Great Depression

Directions Complete this graphic organizer by making inferences about the Great Depression.

FACT		INFERENCE
On October 29, 1929, the stock market crashed.	↗	Because of the stock market crash, the economy did not grow and many people lost their jobs.
FACT		
Because of the crash, many businesses failed.	↘	

FACT		INFERENCE
Because people lost their jobs, they had no money to spend.	↗	**Because manufacturers could not sell their products, factories shut down and more people lost their jobs.**
FACT		
Manufacturers could not sell their goods because people had no money to buy them.	↘	

© Harcourt

14 Test Preparation

Directions Read each question and choose the best answer. Then fill in the circle for the answer you have chosen. Be sure to fill in the circle completely.

1 Which area did the United States gain as a result of the Spanish-American War?
- Ⓐ Alaska
- Ⓑ Hawaii
- Ⓒ Puerto Rico
- Ⓓ Panama Canal

2 One of the main goals of the progressives was to—
- Ⓕ make peace with Germany.
- Ⓖ overcome the Great Depression.
- Ⓗ improve state and local government.
- Ⓙ expand the territory of the United States.

3 Which best describes the Great Migration?
- Ⓐ Many Germans moved to the United States during the 1920s, after World War I.
- Ⓑ Many African Americans moved to northern cities, especially during World War I.
- Ⓒ Many immigrants left cities to find work in the suburbs during the Great Depression.
- Ⓓ Many workers left the United States after losing their jobs during the Great Depression.

4 Langston Hughes was a—
- Ⓕ scientist who helped southern farmers.
- Ⓖ American military leader during World War I.
- Ⓗ government official who purchased Alaska.
- Ⓙ well-known poet of the Harlem Renaissance.

5 The New Deal was Franklin D. Roosevelt's plan to—
- Ⓐ help immigrants adjust to life in the United States.
- Ⓑ organize the American effort to build the Panama Canal.
- Ⓒ support the Allies against the Central Powers in World War I.
- Ⓓ put Americans back to work and end the Great Depression.

© Harcourt

World War II Begins

Directions Below is a list of causes and effects related to World War II. Write each cause and effect in the appropriate place on the chart.

- Germany invades Poland in 1939.

- Dictators rise to power in Germany, Italy, Spain, and the Soviet Union.

- Japan attacks Pearl Harbor.

- The Soviet Union joins with Britain and France to fight the Axis Powers.

CAUSE →	EFFECT
World War I and the economic depression of the 1930s bring hard times to many countries around the world.	Dictators rise to power in Germany, Italy, Spain, and the Soviet Union.
Japan attacks Pearl Harbor.	**The United States declares war on Japan.**
Germany invades Poland in 1939.	**France and Britain declare war on Germany, and World War II begins.**
Germany invades the Soviet Union.	The Soviet Union joins with Britain and France to fight the Axis Powers.

© Harcourt

READING SKILLS
Predict a Historical Outcome

Directions The flow chart below lists the steps for predicting a likely outcome. Follow the steps to predict the effects of the end of World War II on the United States economy.

THINK ABOUT WHAT YOU ALREADY KNOW.

At the end of World War I, the United States economy prospered. In the years that followed, new consumer products appeared on the market, and new forms of entertainment became part of American life.

REVIEW NEW INFORMATION YOU HAVE LEARNED.

During World War II, most Americans were able to find good jobs and contribute to the economy.

MAKE A PREDICTION.

The United States economy might also have prospered following World War II.

READ OR GATHER MORE INFORMATION.

Does the new information support my prediction?

Do I need to change my prediction?

GO THROUGH THE STEPS AGAIN IF NECESSARY.

© Harcourt

Name ______________________ Date ______________

Americans and the War

Directions **During World War II Americans at home were told to "Use it up, wear it out, make it do, or do without." Write a paragraph that explains the meaning of this motto and the reasons Americans were encouraged to do this during the war.**

Students should note that the motto refers to Americans' behavior as consumers during World War II. Food, metals, fuel, and consumer goods were in short supply. The motto encouraged Americans to support rationing, to conserve the goods and resources that they had, and to recycle. This allowed more goods and resources to be devoted to the war effort.

Name _____ Date _____

CITIZENSHIP SKILLS
Make Economic Choices

Directions Imagine you have $25 to spend. You must choose between a savings bond which will increase in value after a certain number of years or one of two items you would like to buy. Complete the graphic organizer below to help you make an economic choice.

CHOICES

List two $25 items you would like to buy.

United States savings bond

Students may list any 2 items that each cost about $25.

_____

_____

OPPORTUNITY COSTS

Each item costs $25. The savings bond will soon be worth $50.

Buying a savings bond would keep you from buying something else you might want.

The opportunity cost is the $25 you will not earn if you choose not to buy the savings bond.

ECONOMIC CHOICE

Compare the value of what you will be giving up, or the opportunity costs, for each choice. When you have made your decision, your other choices become your trade-offs.

Students should list one of the three items.
_____

© Harcourt

Winning the War

Directions Use the terms below to solve the crossword puzzle.

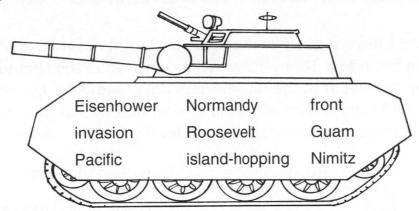

Eisenhower	Normandy	front
invasion	Roosevelt	Guam
Pacific	island-hopping	Nimitz

Across

3 Ocean that surrounds Hawaii

4 D day landing site

7 Allies' plan for defeating Japan

Down

1 Action taken by Allies on D day

2 Commander of Allied troops in Europe

4 American admiral in the Pacific

5 President of the United States during most of World War II

6 Battle line

8 Important Pacific island captured by Allied troops

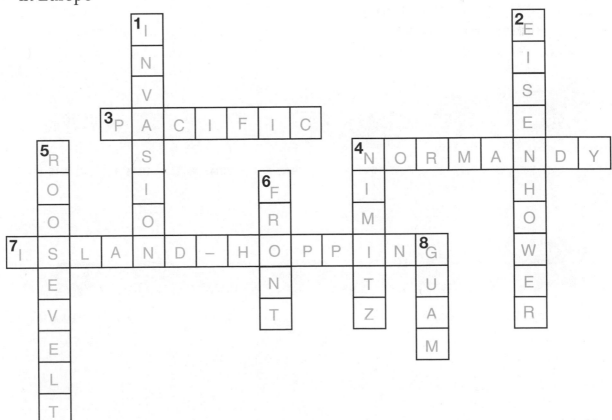

© Harcourt

Use after reading Chapter 15, Lesson 3, pages 565–569.

CHART AND GRAPH SKILLS
Read Parallel Time Lines

Directions Find the year each of the following events took place. Write the year in the space provided. Then, if the event occurred in the United States, write the letter of the event at the appropriate date below the *Events at Home* time line. Write the letters of all the events that occurred outside the United States at the appropriate date below the *Events Overseas* time line.

__1943__ **A.** Allies push Germany out of North Africa.

__1940__ **B.** Japan invades Indochina.

__1944__ **C.** American troops capture Rome.

__1945__ **D.** President Roosevelt dies.

__1941__ **E.** President Roosevelt gives the "Date of Infamy" speech.

__1943__ **F.** American factories produce almost 86,000 aircraft.

__1945__ **G.** Germany surrenders.

__1939__ **H.** Germany invades Poland.

__1942__ **I.** Japanese Americans are forced to move to relocation camps.

__1944__ **J.** Allies launch D day invasion.

__1944__ **K.** Americans elect Franklin D. Roosevelt for a fourth term as President.

__1945__ **L.** Japan surrenders.

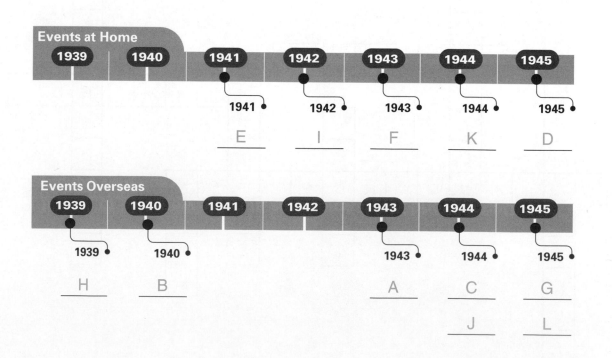

Use after reading Chapter 15, Skill Lesson, pages 570–571.

© Harcourt

The Effects of War

Directions Write each effect of World War II in the appropriate column of the table below.

- Germany's land is divided among Britain, France, the Soviet Union, and the United States.

- Nazi leaders are tried for their crimes at Nuremberg.

- More than 12 million people die in Nazi concentration camps; about half are European Jews.

- The Cold War begins.

- Europe and Japan begin rebuilding cities destroyed in the war.

- Representatives from 50 countries form the United Nations.

- The Soviet Union sets up communist governments in Eastern Europe.

- The United States introduces the Marshall Plan.

Effects of World War II		
The Holocaust	**Plans for Peace**	**A Changed World**
More than 12 million people die in Nazi concentration camps; about half are European Jews.	Europe and Japan begin rebuilding cities destroyed in the war.	The Soviet Union sets up communist governments in Eastern Europe.
Nazi leaders are tried for their crimes at Nuremberg.	Germany's land is divided among Britain, France, the Soviet Union, and the United States.	The United States introduces the Marshall Plan.
	Representatives from 50 countries form the United Nations.	The Cold War begins.

Use after reading Chapter 15, Lesson 4, pages 572–575.

World War II and the United States

Directions Complete this graphic organizer by determining the causes and effects of the involvement of the United States in World War II.

CAUSE

The Japanese attack Pearl Harbor.

EFFECT

19 American ships are sunk or damaged and 150 planes are destroyed.

EFFECT

The United States enters World War II.

EFFECT

2,000 sailors and soldiers are killed in the attack.

CAUSE

The United States joins the Allied forces.

EFFECT

15 million Americans serve in the armed forces during the war.

EFFECT

Food, fuel, and metals are rationed and the production of many consumer goods is stopped.

EFFECT

Because of the need for large amounts of wartime materials, many people now have jobs.

Use after reading Chapter 15, pages 553–575.

Name _____ Date _____

15 Test Preparation

Directions Read each question and choose the best answer. Then fill in the circle for the answer you have chosen. Be sure to fill in the circle completely.

1 Who became dictator of the Soviet Union in 1924?
- Ⓐ Adolf Hitler
- **Ⓑ Joseph Stalin**
- Ⓒ Francisco Franco
- Ⓓ Benito Mussolini

2 By the end of 1941, Germany had taken over—
- Ⓕ Pearl Harbor.
- Ⓖ much of China.
- **Ⓗ much of Europe.**
- Ⓙ Britain and Canada.

3 During World War II, many American women held jobs as—
- Ⓐ fighter pilots.
- Ⓑ wheat farmers.
- **Ⓒ factory workers.**
- Ⓓ cattle ranchers.

4 What strategy did the Allies use to defeat Japan in the Pacific?
- Ⓕ the Marshall Plan
- Ⓖ *Blitzkrieg*
- Ⓗ relocation
- **Ⓙ island-hopping**

5 Why did the Soviet Union join the Allies?
- **Ⓐ Germany attempted an invasion of the Soviet Union.**
- Ⓑ Japan launched a surprise attack against the Soviet Union.
- Ⓒ The Soviet Union wanted to support other communist nations.
- Ⓓ The Allies offered the Soviet Union aid from the Marshall Plan.

© Harcourt

Name _____   Date _____

The Early Years of the Cold War

Directions In the space provided, write the year each of the following events took place. Then write the number of each event in the appropriate place on the time line.

1 ___1952___ Americans elect Dwight D. Eisenhower as President.

2 ___1949___ China becomes a communist country.

3 ___1958___ Congress sets up NASA.

4 ___1959___ Cuba becomes a communist country.

5 ___1961___ East Germany builds a wall to stop its citizens from leaving.

6 ___1963___ Lyndon Johnson becomes President of the United States.

7 ___1950___ North Korea invades South Korea.

8 ___1963___ President Kennedy is assassinated.

9 ___1948___ South Korea becomes a republic; North Korea becomes a communist country.

10 ___1948___ The Soviet Union cuts Berlin off from West Germany.

11 ___1957___ The Soviet Union launches *Sputnik,* the first space satellite.

12 ___1962___ The United States blockades Cuba to force it to remove Soviet missiles.

13 ___1969___ United States astronaut Neil Armstrong becomes the first human to walk on the moon.

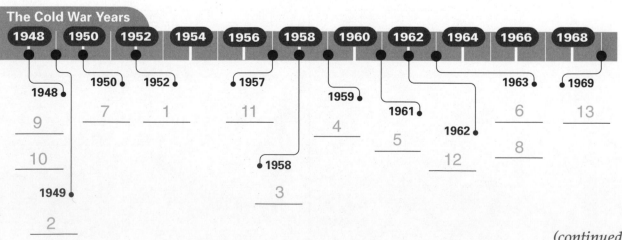

© Harcourt

(continued)

Name _____ Date _____

Directions Use the information from the time line on the previous page to decide whether each statement below is true or false. If the statement is true, write a *T* next to the statement. If the statement is false, write an *F* and explain why the statement is false.

__F__ **14** North Korea became a communist country by following the example set by Cuba. North Korea became a communist country 11 years before Cuba did.

__F__ **15** Congress set up NASA in response to the Soviet blockade of Berlin. The Berlin blockade occurred ten years before Congress set up NASA. Congress acted in response to the launch of *Sputnik*.

__F__ **16** President Johnson tried to stop China from becoming a communist country. By the time Johnson became President in 1963, China had been a communist nation for 14 years.

__T__ **17** The United States was the first nation to land a person on the moon.

_____

_____

__F__ **18** The Soviet Union launched *Sputnik* to force President Kennedy to back down during the Cuban Missile Crisis. The Soviet Union launched *Sputnik* five years before the Cuban Missile Crisis.

Working for Equal Rights

Directions Use the information below to complete the chart.

- Thurgood Marshall

- This person's refusal to give up a seat on a segregated bus led the United States Supreme Court to rule that public transportation could no longer be segregated.

- This leader fought for the rights of migrant farm workers and helped start a group that became the United Farm Workers.

- Malcolm X

- Cesar Chavez

- This winner of the Nobel Peace Prize helped lead the Montgomery bus boycott, encouraged people to use nonviolent ways to end segregation, and led a famous civil rights march in Washington, D.C.

Civil Rights Activist	Notable Ideas/Accomplishments
Cesar Chavez	This leader led a nationwide boycott of California grapes to convince grape growers to improve the pay and conditions for migrant workers.
Dolores Huerta	This leader fought for the rights of migrant farm workers and helped start a group that became the United Farm Workers.
Martin Luther King, Jr.	This winner of the Nobel Peace Prize helped lead the Montgomery Bus Boycott, encouraged people to use nonviolent ways to end segregation, and led a famous civil rights march in Washington, D.C.
Thurgood Marshall	This lawyer argued and won the case *Brown v. Board of Education of Topeka*, which resulted in a United States Supreme Court ruling that public schools could no longer be segregated.
Rosa Parks	This person's refusal to give up a seat on a segregated bus led the United States Supreme Court to rule that public transportation could no longer be segregated.
Malcolm X	This civil rights leader at first spoke in favor of separation of races, but later talked about racial cooperation.

© Harcourt

Use after reading Chapter 16, Lesson 2, pages 585–589.

Name _____ Date _____

The Cold War Continues

Directions Below is a list of causes and effects related to the Vietnam War. Write each item from the list in the appropriate box on the cause-and-effect chart.

Bombing does not stop North Vietnam from supporting Vietcong

President Nixon signs cease-fire

President Johnson orders bombing of North Vietnam

United States economy suffers

United States wants to stop spread of communism

President Nixon wants to withdraw from Vietnam, but does not want communists to take over South Vietnam

South Vietnam surrenders

United States blockades North Vietnam and increases bombing

CAUSE ➡ **EFFECT**

CAUSE	EFFECT
United States wants to stop spread of communism	**United States supports South Vietnam**
North Vietnam torpedoes United States Navy ship	President Johnson orders bombing of North Vietnam
Bombing does not stop North Vietnam from supporting Vietcong	**United States sends hundreds of thousands of soldiers to help South Vietnam**
United States government raises taxes and borrows money	United States economy suffers
President Nixon wants to withdraw from Vietnam, but does not want communists to take over South Vietnam	**United States begins bringing troops home but also sends some troops to Cambodia to destroy North Vietnam's war supplies**
North Vietnam starts large-scale attack on South Vietnam	United States blockades North Vietnam and increases bombing
President Nixon signs cease-fire	**United States troops come home**
North Vietnam attacks South Vietnam again	South Vietnam surrenders

© Harcourt

Name _____   Date _____

A World of Change

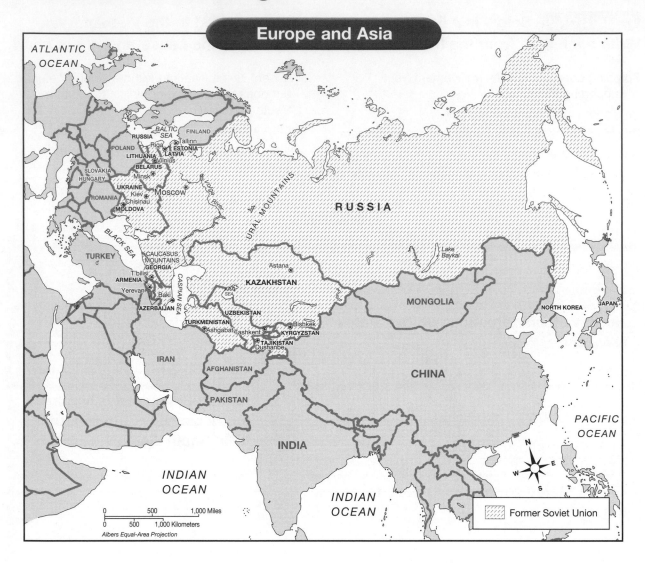

Europe and Asia

ATLANTIC OCEAN

BALTIC SEA

RUSSIA FINLAND
POLAND Riga Tallinn
  LITHUANIA ESTONIA
    Vilnius LATVIA
SLOVAKIA BELARUS
HUNGARY Minsk
  UKRAINE
ROMANIA Kiev Moscow
  Chisinau
MOLDOVA

BLACK SEA

TURKEY CAUCASUS MOUNTAINS
  GEORGIA
  T'bilisi
ARMENIA
  Yerevan Baki
  AZERBAIJAN

URAL MOUNTAINS

RUSSIA

Astana

Lake Baykal

KAZAKHSTAN

CASPIAN SEA

ARAL SEA

UZBEKISTAN
TURKMENISTAN
  Ashgabat Tashkent Bishkek
    KYRGYZSTAN
  TAJIKISTAN
  Dushanbe

MONGOLIA

NORTH KOREA JAPAN

IRAN

AFGHANISTAN

CHINA

PAKISTAN

INDIA

PACIFIC OCEAN

INDIAN OCEAN

INDIAN OCEAN

0   500   1,000 Miles
0   500   1,000 Kilometers
Albers Equal-Area Projection

Former Soviet Union

(continued)

Use after reading Chapter 16, Lesson 4, pages 596–601.

© Harcourt

Name _____ Date _____

1 When the Soviet Union broke up, how many independent countries were

formed? _15_____

2 Which of the former Soviet countries is the largest? _Russia_____

3 Which of the former Soviet countries reaches the farthest south?

Tajikistan _____

4 Which of the former Soviet countries shares a border with China?

Kazakhstan, Kyrgyzstan, Russia, Tajikistan _____

5 Which of the former Soviet countries shares a border with Afghanistan?

Turkmenistan, Uzbekistan, Tajikistan _____

6 Which of the former Soviet countries has access to the Black Sea?

Georgia, Russia, Ukraine _____

7 Which body of water is at the southern end of the Volga River?

the Caspian Sea _____

8 What is the capital of Uzbekistan? _Tashkent_____

9 Of the countries that were formerly part of the Soviet Union, which has the

northernmost capital? _Estonia_____

10 Which mountains are on the northern border of the Republic of Georgia?

the Caucasus Mountains _____

Name _____   Date _____

MAP AND GLOBE SKILLS
Read a Population Map

Directions   Study the map, and answer the questions below.

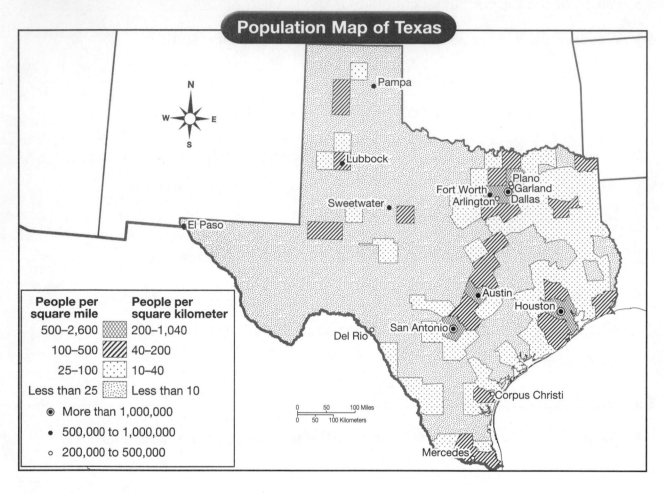

Population Map of Texas

People per square mile	People per square kilometer
500–2,600	200–1,040
100–500	40–200
25–100	10–40
Less than 25	Less than 10
⊙ More than 1,000,000
• 500,000 to 1,000,000
○ 200,000 to 500,000

1 About how many people per square mile live in El Paso?

less than 25

2 About how many people per square mile live in Corpus Christi?

between 100 and 500

3 Do more people live in Plano or in Dallas?   Dallas

4 Which is more populated, East Texas or West Texas?   East Texas

(continued)

Use after reading Chapter 16, Skill Lesson, pages 602–603.

Name _____ Date _____

Population density is the number of people per unit of area, such as "100 people per square mile." Population density describes how crowded an area is. To calculate population density, divide the total number of people by the total area of land. For example, the United States has a population of about 291 million and is 3,717,796 square miles in area.

Population ÷ Area = Population Density
291,000,000 ÷ *3,717,796* = about 78 people per square mile

To do this on a calculator:

enter *291000000*   press ÷   enter *3717796*   press =

Directions **Calculate the population densities of the nations listed below.**

5 Australia's population is 18,783,551 people, and its area is 2,967,900 square miles.

_____18,783,551_____ ÷ _____2,967,900_____ = _____about 6_____ people per square mile
(population)   *(area)*   *(population density)*

6 The United Kingdom's population is 59,113,439 people, and its area is 94,500 square miles

_____59,113,439_____ ÷ _____94,500_____ = _____about 626_____ people per square mile
(population)   *(area)*   *(population density)*

7 Russia's population is 146,393,569 people, and its area is 6,592,800 square miles.

_____146,393,569_____ ÷ _____6,592,800_____ = _____about 22_____ people per square mile
(population)   *(area)*   *(population density)*

8 Japan's population is 126,182,077 people, and its area is 145,882 square miles.

_____126,182,077_____ ÷ _____145,882_____ = _____about 865_____ people per square mile
(population)   *(area)*   *(population density)*

© Harcourt

Use after reading Chapter 16, Skill Lesson, pages 602–603.   **Activity Book** ▪ **157**

Name _____ Date _____

The Cold War and the End of the Soviet Union

Directions Complete this graphic organizer by filling in facts and outcomes about the Cold War.

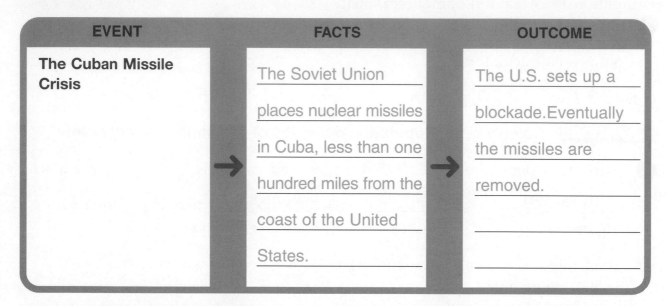

EVENT	FACTS	OUTCOME
The Cuban Missile Crisis	The Soviet Union places nuclear missiles in Cuba, less than one hundred miles from the coast of the United States.	The U.S. sets up a blockade. Eventually the missiles are removed.

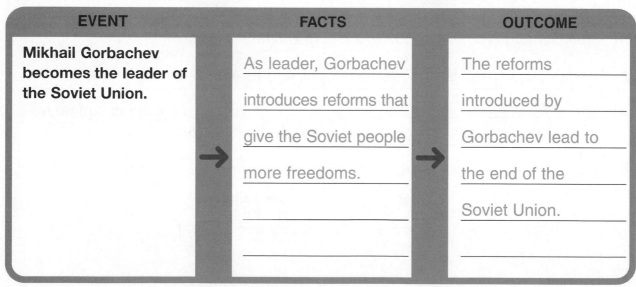

EVENT	FACTS	OUTCOME
Mikhail Gorbachev becomes the leader of the Soviet Union.	As leader, Gorbachev introduces reforms that give the Soviet people more freedoms.	The reforms introduced by Gorbachev lead to the end of the Soviet Union.

Use after reading Chapter 16, pages 578–603.

© Harcourt

16 Test Preparation

Directions Read each question and choose the best answer. Then fill in the circle for the answer you have chosen. Be sure to fill in the circle completely.

1 In an arms race, nations compete to—
- Ⓐ sell the most weapons.
- Ⓑ use the most weapons.
- Ⓒ build the most weapons.
- Ⓓ destroy the most weapons.

2 In the case *Brown v. Board of Education of Topeka,* the United States Supreme Court decided that—
- Ⓕ all cities must set up public school systems.
- Ⓖ segregation on school buses is unconstitutional.
- Ⓗ segregated schools cannot offer an equal education.
- Ⓙ all teachers must receive equal pay, no matter what their race is.

3 Sandra Day O'Connor was the first woman to—
- Ⓐ orbit Earth and walk on the moon.
- Ⓑ run for President of the United States.
- Ⓒ serve as a United States Supreme Court justice.
- Ⓓ fight for the rights of migrant workers.

4 What was the Great Society?
- Ⓕ an organization that fought for civil rights for African Americans
- Ⓖ President Johnson's plan to improve the lives of Americans
- Ⓗ the United States' strategy to force Cuba to get rid of its Soviet missiles
- Ⓙ an organization that encouraged people to visit the United States

5 How did President George Bush respond when Iraq invaded Kuwait?
- Ⓐ He pulled all United States troops out of Vietnam.
- Ⓑ He convinced the leaders of Egypt and Israel to sign a peace treaty.
- Ⓒ He called Iraq "an evil empire."
- Ⓓ He organized Operation Desert Storm.

© Harcourt

Use after reading Chapter 16, pages 580–603.

Name _____ Date _____

The Twentieth Century

Directions Read the statements about Canada and Mexico, and identify each as a fact or an opinion. Write F if the statement is a fact and O if the statement is an opinion.

1. ___F___ Many of Mexico's maquiladoras, or assembly plants, are located along the border with the United States.

2. ___F___ Canadian women gained the right to vote two years before women in the United States did.

3. ___O___ The Mexican economy is better today because half of all Mexican jobs are in service industries.

4. ___F___ Mexico's oil deposits helped diversify the Mexican economy.

5. ___O___ Canadians should enjoy living in a nation in which both English and French are official languages.

6. ___O___ President Porfirio Díaz was Mexico's harshest president.

7. ___O___ The Canadian government is right to protect the cultures of the Native Canadians.

8. ___F___ Canada planned to play a limited role in World War II, but heavy casualties led the Canadian government to create a large army.

9. ___F___ Mexico worries that too many of its people are moving to the United States.

10. ___F___ Canada's secondary industries involve the processing of natural resources and finished products.

© Harcourt

Name _____   Date _____

Directions An outline is a list that organizes information about a topic. It shows how important ideas relate to one another. Study the outline about United States involvement in Central America and the Caribbean. Use your textbook to help you fill in the missing information.

I. **The United States and Panama**
   A. United States Military Involvement in Panama
      1. The United States military helped Panama win independence from Colombia.
      2. Panama remained under the military protection of the United States until 1936.
      3. The United States military arrested Panama's dictator, General Mañuel Noriega.
   B. The Panama Canal
      1. Panama gave the United States a strip of land on which to build the Panama Canal.
      2. In 1977, the United States agreed to return the Canal Zone to Panama in the year 2000.
      3. The United States returned the Canal Zone on December 31, 1999.

II. **The United States, Nicaragua, and El Salvador**
   A. United States Involvement in Central American Civil Wars
      1. In the 1980s the United States gave economic and military aid to the government of El Salvador to fight Communist rebels.
      2. The United States secretly supported the Contras, who fought Nicaragua's Communist government.

III. **The United States and Haiti**
   A. United States Involvement in Haiti
      1. The United States military restored order in Haiti during World War I and remained until 1934.
      2. The United States controlled Haitian finances until 1947.
      3. In 1994 the United States invaded Haiti to allow democratically elected president Jean-Bertrand Aristide to return to power.

© Harcourt

The American People Today

Directions Choose two of the items shown. Write a paragraph explaining the effect that each item has had on life in the United States. Describe what life might be like without the item. Students' answers may vary; possible answers are given.

Cellular telephone—Effect: helps people stay connected; makes communications/

businesses move faster. Without: would be harder to reach people when they were

away from home or office. Personal computer—Effect: allows people to complete

many tasks, even run businesses from home; allows people to connect via Internet

and World Wide Web to sources of information around the world; allows instant

sharing of documents, images, and sounds via e-mail. Without: would have to

physically travel to accomplish many tasks (shopping, banking, researching); sharing

information would take longer. Air conditioner—Effect: spurred population and

economic growth and environmental change in the Sun Belt by making life there

more comfortable. Without: population of South would probably be much smaller;

population of West would probably not be fastest-growing in the United States.

© Harcourt

(continued)

Use after reading Chapter 17, Lesson 1, pages 620–625.

Name _____ Date _____

Directions Use the clues to complete the word puzzle. The letters in the outlined box will spell a word that describes a characteristic of the United States population.

Clues

1 Many people who come to live in the United States are looking for _____ and opportunity.

2 More than 1 million _____ came to the United States during the 1990s.

3 The United States population grows when more people are born and when more people _____ to this country.

4 The Sun _____ stretches across the southern United States.

5 Texas and _____ have the largest Hispanic populations.

6 Currently, most people who come to live in the United States are from Latin American or _____ countries.

7 Of the 20 percent of United States school children who do not speak English at home, most speak _____.

8 A group of people from the same country, of the same race, or with the same culture is called a(n) _____ group.

9 A decade is a period of ten _____.

```
¹F  R  E  E │D│ O  M
      ²I  M  M │I│ G  R  A  N  T  S
         ³M  O │V│ E
            ⁴B │E│ L  T
⁵C  A  L  I  F  O │R│ N  I  A
            ⁶A │S│ I  A  N
   ⁷S  P  A  N │I│ S  H
            ⁸E │T│ H  N  I  C
               ⁹Y │E│ A  R  S
```

Use after reading Chapter 17, Lesson 1, pages 620–625.

CHART AND GRAPH SKILLS
Use a Cartogram

The cartogram below shows the population of North America.

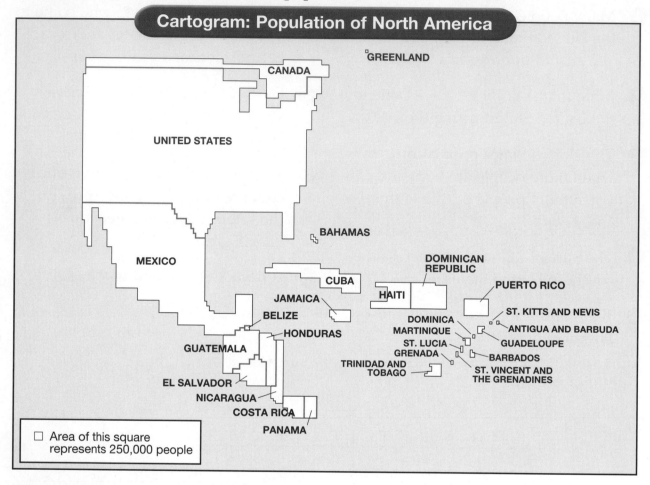

Cartogram: Population of North America

GREENLAND

CANADA

UNITED STATES

MEXICO

BAHAMAS

DOMINICAN REPUBLIC

CUBA

HAITI

PUERTO RICO

JAMAICA

BELIZE

ST. KITTS AND NEVIS

HONDURAS

DOMINICA

ANTIGUA AND BARBUDA

MARTINIQUE

GUATEMALA

ST. LUCIA

GUADELOUPE

GRENADA

BARBADOS

EL SALVADOR

TRINIDAD AND TOBAGO

ST. VINCENT AND THE GRENADINES

NICARAGUA

COSTA RICA

PANAMA

☐ Area of this square represents 250,000 people

Directions Write a brief paragraph that defines the term *population cartogram,* and discusses appropriate and inappropriate uses of a population cartogram.

Definition: The size of each geographical area represents the size of the population

of the area rather than the physical size of the area.

Appropriate: to compare populations of various locations

Inappropriate: to determine distances between locations

(continued)

Use after reading Chapter 17, Skill Lesson, pages 626–627.

© Harcourt

Name _____   Date _____

Directions Use the population cartogram of North America on the previous page and a political map of North America from your textbook to answer the following questions. Remember that Puerto Rico is a territory of the United States.

1 Which country has the largest population? United States _____

2 What country has the second largest population? Mexico _____

3 Which country has the greatest land area? Canada _____

4 Which country has the smaller population, Cuba or Jamaica?

Jamaica _____

5 Which is larger: the population of Canada or the population of Mexico?

Mexico _____

6 Which country has the larger population, Costa Rica or Belize?

Costa Rica _____

7 Which two countries have the largest populations? United States and Mexico

_____

8 What does the size of Mexico on the cartogram tell you about the population of

Mexico? that Mexico has a large population _____

9 What does the size of Canada on the cartogram and on the map tell you about

the population of Canada? that Canada does not have a very large population

_____

Name _____   Date _____

The Challenges of Growth

Directions The table shows six challenges that face a growing population. Write each solution from the list below in the appropriate box in the table. Some challenges will have more than one solution. Some solutions may help solve more than one challenge.

Solutions

add more bus routes

adjust number of seats in Congress to match current states' populations

build rapid-transit systems

pass laws to protect endangered species

improve public transportation

prevent building on some land

recycle glass, metal, plastic, and paper

use electronic highway signs

use computer-controlled traffic lights

pass laws to stop land and water pollution

improve technology

Challenges	Solutions
1 Damage to wildlife	pass laws to protect endangered species; pass laws to stop land and water pollution; prevent building on some land
2 Large amounts of trash	recycle glass, metal, plastic, and paper
3 Demands on natural resources	pass laws to stop land and water pollution; recycle glass, metal, plastic, and paper; improve technology
4 Keeping government fair	adjust number of seats in Congress to match current states' populations
5 Roads jammed with cars and trucks	add more bus routes; build rapid-transit systems; use computer-controlled traffic lights; use electronic highway signs; improve public transportation

© Harcourt

Use after reading Chapter 17, Lesson 2, pages 628–631.

The American Economy

Directions Use the terms from the lesson to solve the crossword puzzle.

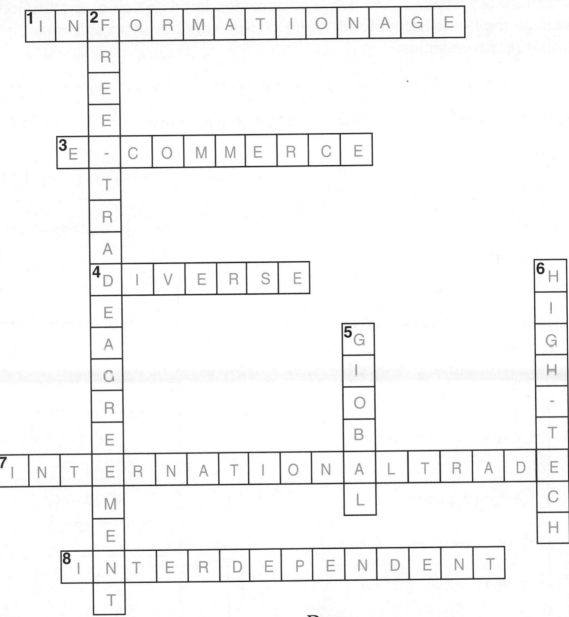

Across

1. A period when people can find and share rapidly-growing knowledge
3. Buying products on the Internet
4. An economy that is not based on just one kind of industry
7. Buying and selling between companies in more than one country
8. Businesses that rely on each other for resources, products, or services

Down

2. A promise between nations not to tax the products that they buy from or sell to each other
5. An economy that includes businesses from around the world
6. Businesses that design, produce, or use electronic equipment

Use after reading Chapter 17, Lesson 3, pages 632–637.

Government and the People

Directions Complete the Web page below by filling in certain responsibilities of United States citizens. The home page on the left lists some constitutional rights. Use the items below to fill in the pop-up windows with citizens' matching responsibilities.

• Stay informed about local, state, and national events; respect the views of others

• Register and take part in local, state, and national elections

• Treat others fairly

• Be willing to serve on a jury

Responsibilities of Citizens

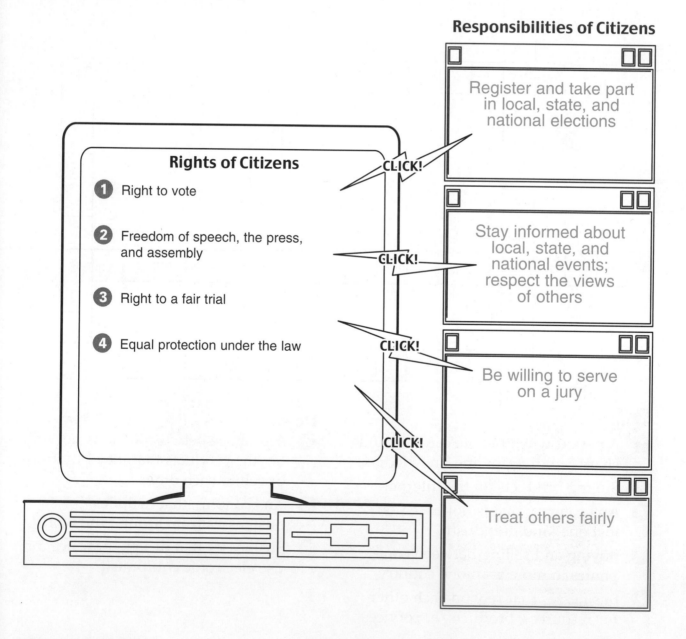

Rights of Citizens

1 Right to vote

2 Freedom of speech, the press, and assembly

3 Right to a fair trial

4 Equal protection under the law

CLICK!

CLICK!

CLICK!

CLICK!

Register and take part in local, state, and national elections

Stay informed about local, state, and national events; respect the views of others

Be willing to serve on a jury

Treat others fairly

© Harcourt

Use after reading Chapter 17, Lesson 4, pages 638–643.

CITIZENSHIP SKILLS
Identify Political Symbols

Directions Match each symbol below with the appropriate description. Write the letter of the description on the line next to the symbol. Some descriptions will be used more than once.

1 _e_

2 _a_

a. United States government

b. Democratic party

c. United States Congress

d. Republican party

e. President of the United States

f. The United States of America

g. freedom

3 _d_

6 _b_

4 _f_

7 _c_

5 _f_

8 _g_

© Harcourt

Facts and Opinions About the United States

Directions Complete this graphic organizer by identifying facts and opinions about the United States.

THE POPULATION OF THE UNITED STATES

FACT

More than 291 million people live in the United States.

OPINION

Student answers will vary. Sample answer: The larger the population of the United States, the better.

FACT

Most immigrants come to the United States seeking freedom and a better way of life.

OPINION

Student answers will vary. Sample answer: The United States is one of the best countries to live in.

THE UNITED STATES GOVERNMENT AND THE PEOPLE

FACT

Citizens who feel strongly about an issue can contact their representative by making phone calls.

OPINION

Student answers will vary. Sample answer: If you feel strongly about an issue, you should call your representative.

FACT

Today e-mail makes staying in touch with government leaders simpler than ever.

OPINION

Student answers will vary. Sample answer: Because communicating with government leaders has become so easy, Americans should take a more active role in their government.

© Harcourt

Name _____ Date _____

17 Test Preparation

Directions Read each question and choose the best answer. Then fill in the circle for the answer you have chosen. Be sure to fill in the circle completely.

1 Today, from where do most immigrants to the United States come?
- Ⓐ Asia and Europe
- Ⓑ Africa and Europe
- Ⓒ Asia and Latin America
- Ⓓ Africa and Latin America

2 How can a rapid-transit system prevent traffic jams?
- Ⓕ by providing people with alternate ways to travel
- Ⓖ by adding traffic lights to highways
- Ⓗ by adding more highways
- Ⓙ by limiting the number of people who travel by train

3 Which is an example of a service job?
- Ⓐ miner
- Ⓑ nurse
- Ⓒ farmer
- Ⓓ factory worker

4 In a free-enterprise economy, which is a result of an increased demand for a product?
- Ⓕ The price of the product will go up.
- Ⓖ The product's price will be set by the government.
- Ⓗ Fewer people will want to buy the product.
- Ⓙ Fewer companies will want to sell the product.

5 What is the role of the federal government?
- Ⓐ To organize the two main political parties
- Ⓑ To oversee the work of the state governments
- Ⓒ To stop local laws from conflicting with state laws
- Ⓓ To make and apply the laws that run the United States

© Harcourt

Use after reading Chapter 17, pages 618–649.

Mexico

Directions Write the letter next to each event listed below in the appropriate place on the time line.

a. In the early 1900s, Mexican leaders write a new constitution that includes land for farmers and a six-year limit on presidents' terms.

b. Soon after the Mexican economy starts to recover, Mexico elects its first president from the Partido Acción Nacional (PAN), Vicente Fox.

c. United States President George W. Bush meets with Mexican President Vicente Fox to show the importance of ties between the two nations.

d. In the late 1900s Mexico, Canada, and the United States sign the North American Free Trade Agreement (NAFTA).

e. In the 1820s part of Spain's army helps Mexico win its independence.

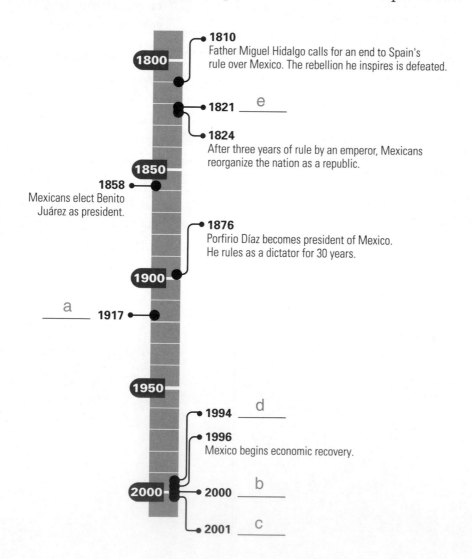

1810
Father Miguel Hidalgo calls for an end to Spain's rule over Mexico. The rebellion he inspires is defeated.

1821 ___e___

1824
After three years of rule by an emperor, Mexicans reorganize the nation as a republic.

1858
Mexicans elect Benito Juárez as president.

1876
Porfirio Díaz becomes president of Mexico. He rules as a dictator for 30 years.

___a___ **1917**

1994 ___d___

1996
Mexico begins economic recovery.

2000 ___b___

2001 ___c___

© Harcourt

Use after reading Chapter 18, Lesson 1, pages 652–656.

Central America and the Caribbean

Directions Answer the questions below.

1 What seven countries make up Central America? Belize, Guatemala, Honduras, El Salvador, Nicaragua, Costa Rica, Panama

2 What crops are grown in the countries of Central America?
bananas, beans, coffee, corn, cotton, and sugarcane

3 Which natural events challenge the residents of islands in the Caribbean?
volcanic eruptions, earthquakes, tropical storms, hurricanes, droughts, heavy rains, mudslides, and flooding

4 What kind of government does Cuba have? a communist dictatorship

5 Which Caribbean islands are part of the United States? Puerto Rico, the Virgin Islands

6 How is the government of Costa Rica similar to the government of the United States? It is a democracy with three branches of government and a president elected to a four-year term.

CHART AND GRAPH SKILLS
Read Population Pyramids

Directions Study the population pyramid of Costa Rica below. Then write a paragraph that explains to another student what the pyramid reveals about the population of Costa Rica. As you write, try to answer these questions:

1 What is a population pyramid?

2 Which part of the pyramid is the largest? What does this mean?

3 Which part of the pyramid is the smallest? What does this mean?

4 Does the pyramid show any differences between females and males?

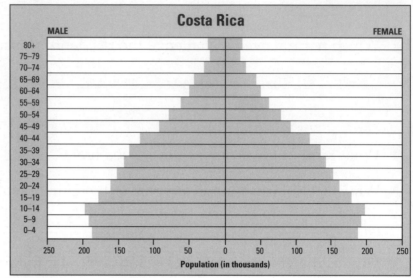

Source: U.S. Census Bureau, International Data Base.

5 About how many Costa Ricans are in your age group?

Students' paragraphs should include the following:

1) A population pyramid shows the division of a country's population by age

and sex.   2) The largest part is males and females aged 10–14. There are more

people in this group than in any other group in Costa Rica.   3) The smallest

part is males aged 75–79. This is the smallest population group in Costa

Rica. 4) There are more young men than young women in Costa Rica, about the

same number of middle-aged men and women, and slightly more older women

than men.   5) For 10-year olds: more than 400,000 people in age group; for

9-year olds: about 400,000 people in age group

(continued)

© Harcourt

Name _____ Date _____

Directions The population pyramid on the left represents the population of Mexico in 1980. The population pyramid on the right illustrates what the Mexican population might look like in 2030. Use the information from the two pyramids to answer the questions below.

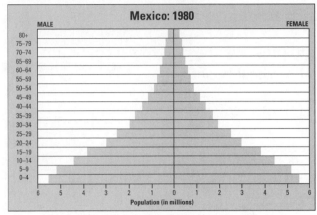

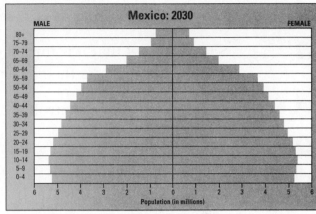

Source: U.S. Census Bureau, International Data Base. Source: U.S. Census Bureau, International Data Base.

6 About how many people were 20–24 years old in 1980? _about 6 million_

in 2030? _about 10 million_

7 Which age group was the smallest in 1980? _80+ years old_

in 2030? _80+ years old_

8 Which age group was the largest in 1980? _0–4 years old_

in 2030? _10–14 years old_

9 What is the predicted approximate increase in the number of people 50–54 years old between 1980 and 2030? _about 6 million_

10 Do any gender/age groups show a predicted decrease between 1980 and 2030?

yes

If so, which one(s)? _males and females 0–4 years old_

11 About how many people were less than 15 years old in 1980?

about 30 million

© Harcourt

South America

Directions Read each statement below. If the statement is true, write *T* in the blank. If the statement is false, write *F* in the blank.

1 __F__ Most of South America is covered in tropical rain forest.

2 __T__ Scientists feel that it is important to preserve the rain forests of South America because of their potential medical benefits.

3 __F__ At one time Spain controlled all of South America.

4 __F__ All *mestizos* come from South America.

5 __T__ The American and French revolutions encouraged people in South American colonies to fight for their independence.

6 __T__ Simón Bolívar was one of the leaders of the efforts to free South American colonies.

7 __F__ Simón Bolívar believed that the former South American colonies had so much in common that they could join together as a single nation.

8 __T__ In the new, independent countries of South America, dictators or armies often took control of the political process.

9 __T__ Reformers in South America have worked to help small farmers own their land.

Use after reading Chapter 18, Lesson 3, pages 664–668.

© Harcourt

Canada

Directions Circle the letter of the best answer.

1 Which best represents the flag of Canada?

A.    B.    C.    D.

2 Which is a prairie province of Canada?

F. Alberta   H. Ontario

G. Quebec   J. Nunavut

3 Which ocean does **not** border Canada?

A. Arctic   C. Pacific

B. Indian   D. Atlantic

4 Which best describes the relationship between Canada and Great Britain right after the North America Act of 1867?

F. Independent nation   H. Commonwealth partner

G. Conquered territory   J. Representative government

5 Who is the official leader of the executive branch of the Canadian government?

A. The Parliament   C. The British monarch

B. The Prime Minister   D. The governor-general

6 Who runs the executive branch of the Canadian government on a day-to-day basis?

F. The Parliament   H. The British monarch

G. The Prime Minister   J. The governor-general

7 Which nation buys the majority of Canada's exports?

A. France   C. Great Britain

B. Australia   D. the United States

Use after reading Chapter 18, Lesson 4, pages 669–673.

MAP AND GLOBE SKILLS
Use a Time Zone Map

Directions Use the time zone map below to answer the questions.

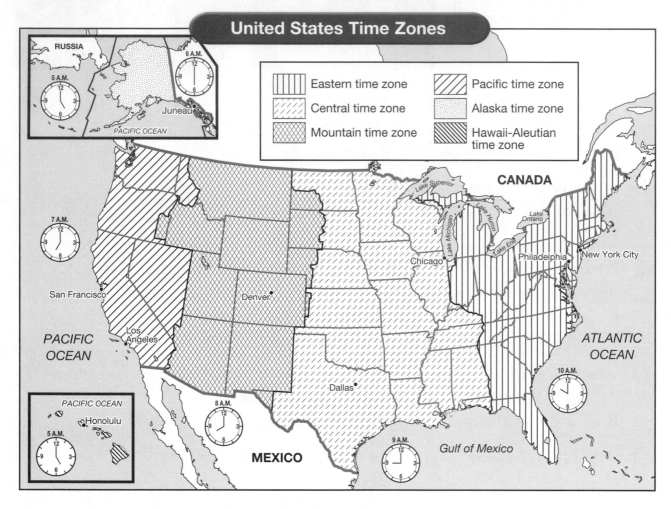

United States Time Zones

Eastern time zone   Pacific time zone

Central time zone   Alaska time zone

Mountain time zone   Hawaii-Aleutian time zone

1 How many time zones cover the 50 states? 6 _____

2 Which of these cities are in the Central time zone: Chicago, Dallas, Denver?

Chicago, Dallas _____

3 When it is 8:00 A.M. in New York City, what time is it in Los Angeles?

5:00 A.M. _____

4 When it is 3:30 P.M. in Chicago, what time is it in Honolulu?

11:30 A.M. _____

(continued)

Name _____ Date _____

Use the time zone map to complete the chart below.

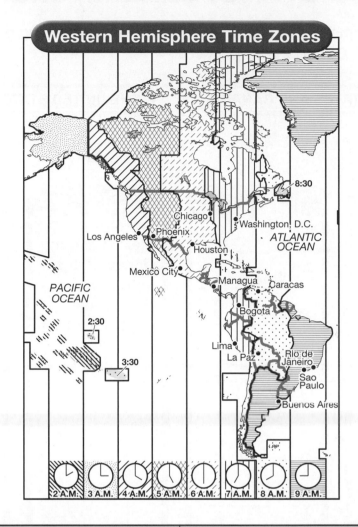

Western Hemisphere Time Zones

When the time is . . .	The time is . . .
5 2:00 A.M. in Buenos Aires	11:00 P.M. in Chicago
6 1:00 P.M. in São Paulo	12:00 P.M. in La Paz
7 6:30 A.M. in Los Angeles	9:30 A.M. in Lima
8 3:45 P.M. in Houston	4:45 P.M. in Bogotá
9 2:00 P.M. in Rio de Janeiro	10:00 A.M. in Phoenix
10 11:30 A.M. in Managua	11:30 A.M. in Mexico City
11 9:15 P.M. in Caracas	8:15 P.M. in Washington, D.C.

Use after reading Chapter 18, Skill Lesson, pages 674–675.

© Harcourt

Name _____ Date _____

The United States, Canada, and Mexico

Directions Complete this graphic organizer by comparing and contrasting the United States, Canada, and Mexico.

THE UNITED STATES AND CANADA	THE UNITED STATES AND MEXICO

SIMILARITIES	DIFFERENCES	SIMILARITIES	DIFFERENCES
Both Canada and the United States were once under British rule.	Today, Canada's executive branch is still headed by Britain's monarch while the United States government is fully independent.	**Mexico and the United States both have democratic governments.**	The president of Mexico can serve only one six-year term, but the President of the United States can serve two four-year terms.

Use after reading Chapter 18, pages 651–677.

© Harcourt

Name _____   Date _____

18 Test Preparation

Directions Read each question and choose the best answer. Then fill in the circle for the answer you have chosen. Be sure to fill in the circle completely.

1 Which two civilizations have created the cultural heritage of Mexico?
- Ⓐ PRI and PAN
- Ⓑ *Mestizo* and French
- Ⓒ Native American and Spanish
- Ⓓ North American and South American

2 Which do many of the Central American and Caribbean nations have in common?
- Ⓕ Land area
- Ⓖ Population size
- Ⓗ Threat of hurricanes
- Ⓙ Communist governments

3 Which word best describes the political history of Haiti?
- Ⓐ Isolated
- Ⓑ Unstable
- Ⓒ Communist
- Ⓓ Democratic

4 Which person led the efforts to free parts of South America from colonial rule?
- Ⓕ Fidel Castro
- Ⓖ Simón Bolívar
- Ⓗ Jean-Bertrand Aristide
- Ⓙ Father Miguel Hidalgo

5 Which two nations in the Western Hemisphere share a border of more than 5,000 miles?
- Ⓐ Colombia and Brazil
- Ⓑ Colombia and Panama
- Ⓒ United States and Mexico
- Ⓓ United States and Canada

© Harcourt

Use after reading Chapter 18, pages 650–677.

Name _____ Date _____

Governments in North America

Directions The governments of Canada and Mexico have both similarities and differences. Read each of the statements below. Then place a check mark to show which country the statement describes. Check both boxes if the statement describes both countries.

	Canada	Mexico
1 The Parliament is made up of two houses— the House of Commons and the Senate.	✔	
2 The chief executive officer is a president who sets policies, influences lawmaking, and plans the budget.		✔
3 The Senate studies issues and makes suggestions but does not enact laws.	✔	
4 The highest court, the Supreme Court, decides if the country's laws are fair.	✔	✔
5 A constitution established the form of the government and the citizens' rights.	✔	✔
6 A premier heads the legislative and executive branches of the country's ten provincial governments.	✔	
7 The Senate has 128 senators. The citizens of 31 states and the Federal District elect 96 of the senators.		✔
8 Some members of the Chamber of Deputies are elected by a system called proportional representation.		✔
9 The leader of the political party with the most seats in the House of Commons becomes the prime minister.	✔	
10 The state governments are made up of one-house legislatures and governors who have few responsibilities.		✔

© Harcourt

Use after reading Unit 8, pages U8-1 to U8-15.

Name _____   Date _____

Directions There are many different governments in the regions of Central America and the Caribbean. For each of the main ideas listed about the governments, write two supporting details.

Answers will vary; possible answers are listed.

MAIN IDEA ➡	SUPPORTING DETAILS
1 Today all seven Central American countries are democracies.	1. Belize is a parliamentary democracy. 2. Costa Rica, El Salvador, Guatemala, Honduras, Nicaragua, and Panama are all republics like the United States.
2 Cuba's government is different from other Caribbean governments.	1. A single party, the Communist Party of Cuba, controls all parts of Cuban society and government. 2. The Council of State, headed by Fidel Castro, leads the Cuban government.
3 The government of Belize is based on that of Britain.	1. Belize is a parliamentary democracy. 2. It is part of the Commonwealth of Nations.
4 Costa Rica is a good example of democracy in Central America.	1. Costa Rica has free elections, majority rule, and more than one political party. 2. Costa Rica's constitution includes many freedoms, such as freedom of speech, equality before the law, and the right to own property.
5 In the past the countries of Central America have had both limited and unlimited governments.	1. Some countries in Central America became independent democracies modeled on the United States. 2. Dictators often took control of Central American countries and ruled with no limits to their authority.

© Harcourt

Use after reading Unit 8, pages U8-1 to U8-15.